A

FAMILIAR DIGEST

OF ALL THE

PENSION AND BOUNTY LAND LAWS

OF THE

UNITED STATES

NOW IN FORCE, SYSTEMATICALLY ARRANGED:

CONTAINING

ALL THE NECESSARY FORMS OF APPLICATION, DECLARATIONS, CERTIFICATES, POWERS OF ATTORNEY, AFFIDAVITS, EXECUTIVE REGULATIONS, RULES OF EVIDENCE, ETC., COMPILED FROM THE OFFICIAL RECORDS.

By WILLIAM HUNT, Counsellor at Law.

PUBLISHED BY THE AUTHOR.

......

WASHINGTON CITY, D. C.
ROBERT A. WATERS PRINT.
1851.

A FAMILIAR DIGEST

OF ALL THE

PENSION AND BOUNTY LAND LAWS

OF THE

UNITED STATES

NOW IN FORCE, SYSTEMATICALLY ARRANGED:

CONTAINING

ALL THE NECESSARY FORMS OF APPLICATION, DECLARATIONS, CERTIFICATES, POWERS OF ATTORNEY, AFFIDAVITS, EXECUTIVE REGULATIONS, RULES OF EVIDENCE, ETC., COMPILED FROM THE OFFICIAL RECORDS.

BY WILLIAM HUNT, COUNSELLOR AT LAW.

PUBLISHED BY THE AUTHOR.

WASHINGTON CITY, D. C.
ROBERT A. WATERS PRINT.
1851.

DISTRICT OF COLUMBIA, TO WIT:

Be it remembered, that, on the fifth day of December, Anno Domini one thousand eght hundred and fifty, WILLIAM HUNT deposited in this office the title of a work, the title of which is in the words following:

"*A Familiar Digest of all the Pension and Bounty Land Laws of the United States now in force, systematically arranged: containing all the necessary forms of Applications, Declarations, Certificates, Powers of Attorney, Affidavits, Executive Regulations, Rules of Evidence, &c., compiled from the Official Records.*" *By* WILLIAM HUNT, *Counsellor at Law.*

The right whereof he claims as author, in conformity with an act of Congress, entitled "An Act to amend the several acts respecting copy rights."

JNO. A. SMITH, *Clerk of the District.*

In testimony that the foregoing is a true copy from the records of my office, I, JOHN A. SMITH, Clerk of the District Court of the District of Columbia, hereto set my hand, and the seal of said Court, this fifth day of December, 1850.

JNO. A. SMITH, *Clerk.*

LIST OF CONTENTS.

ARMY REVOLUTIONARY PENSIONS.

Widows and Children.

ARMY PENSIONS FOR SERVICES SUBSEQUENT TO THE REVOLUTIOV.

WIDOWS PENSIONS FOR SERVICES OF THEIR HUSBANDS SUBSEQUENT TO THE REVOLUTION.

NAVY PENSIONS.

EXECUTIVE REGULATIONS AND RULES OF EVIDENCE.

FORMS.

BOUNTY LANDS.

MEXICAN WAR BOUNTY LANDS.

FORMS AND REGULATIONS FOR OBTAINING MEXICAN BOUNTY LAND WARRANTS.

ARMY.

REVOLUTIONARY PENSIONS.

CHAPTER I.

All persons disabled in service since the Revolution, are entitled to pensions.

On the 10th of April, 1806, Congress re-enacted that portion of the act of March 16, 1802, by which provision was made for persons who were disabled by known wounds received in the Revolutionary war.

By this act, a commissioned officer was allowed, as a full pension, *one half the monthly pay* which was legally allowed at the time of his incurring the disability; the proportion less than a full pension, to correspond with the proportions of said half pay; no pension, however, to be calculated at a higher rate than the half pay of a Lieutenant Colonel.

The full pension of a non-commissioned officer, soldier, marine, or seaman, was fixed at *five dollars per month*, and less than a full pension in the proportion of five dollars per month.

On the 25th of April, 1808, an act was passed, the fourth section of which provides, that any soldier, whether belonging to the regular army, the militia, or a volunteer corps, called into service under the authority of the United States, and who may have been wounded or disabled *since* the Revolutionary war, while in the line of his duty, in the actual service of the United States, shall be entitled to a pension at the same rate of compensation, and under the regulations of the above act of April 10, 1806.

CHAPTER II.

Increase of Pension of every grade under that of Captain.

On the 24th of April, 1816, an act was passed, the first and second sections of which provided, that all persons of the following ranks at that time, or who may hereafter be placed on the military pension roll of the United States, shall receive for the disabilities of the highest degree, the following sums, per month, in lieu of those to which they were previously entitled, viz:

A First Lieutenant, - - -	$17 00
A Second Lieutenant, - - -	15 00
A Third Lieutenant, - - -	14 00
An Ensign, - - - - -	13 00
A non commissioned officer, musician, or private, - - - - -	8 00

For disabilities of a degree less than the highest, a sum proportionably less.

It was also provided, that nothing in this act should be so construed as to lessen the pension of any person, who, by special provision, is entitled to a higher rate of pension.

CHAPTER III

Pensions to those who served nine months.

By the act of March 18, 1818, officers or privates who served in the Army or Navy during the Revolutionary War, for nine months or longer, and who by reason of their reduced circumstances stood in need of assistance from their country, were allowed pensions: officers $20 per month, non commissioned officers privates, etc., $8 per month. No person was entitled to the provisions of this act until he relinquished all claim to any pension heretofore allowed him by the United States. To obtain the benefit of the act, it was necessary to make a statement, under oath, that the applicant stood in need of assistance.

On the 1st of May, 1820, an act was passed, the first section of which declared, that no person placed on the pension list under the act of March 18, 1818, should, after the reception of that part of the pension which became due in March 4, 1820, continued to receive the pension until he should have exhibited, under oath, a schedule of all his estate and income; after which the Secretary of War was empowered to strike from the pension list under the said act, the name of all pensioners who thus appeared capable of supporting themselves without the assistance of their country. It was provided however, that persons who had been placed on the pension list in consequence of disability, from known wounds received in the Revolutionary War, and who had relinquished such pension in order to avail themselves of the benefits of the act of March 18, 1818, and stricken from the list under this section, should be restored to the pension so relinquished.

CHAPTER IV.

Pensions granted to all Officers who served to the end of the Revolutionary War in the Continental Army.

On the 15th of May, 1828, an act was passed which provided, that the surviving commissioned officers of the Revolutionary Army, in the continental line, who served to the end of the war, and who, by the resolution of October 21, 1780, were entitled to half pay, should receive the amount of *full pay*, according to their rank in the line; the said full pay to commence on the 3rd of March, 1826. Under this act no officer is entitled to receive a larger sum than the pay of a Captain in the said line.

This act also provided, that every surviving non-commissioned officer, musician, or private, in said army, who enlisted therein *for and during the war, and continued in its service until its termination,* and thereby became entitled to receive a reward of $80 under the Resolution of May 15, 1778, should be entitled to receive his *full* monthly pay in said service, the said full pay to commence on the 3rd of March, 1826, and to continue during his natural life.

NOTE.—On May 31, 1830, and on July 14, 1832, acts were passed which declared that pensioners under the preceding act of May 15, 1828, should not be required to relinquish invalid pensions, and if they were disabled, that they might receive both pensions.

CHAPTER V.

Provisions for all who served six months, either in the Army, Militia, or Navy, during the Revolution.

On the 7th of June, 1832, it was enacted, that each of the surviving officers, non-commissioned officers, musicians, soldiers, and Indian spies, who had served in the continental line, or State troops, volunteers, or militia, at one or more terms, a period of two years, during the Revolutionary War, and who were not entitled to any benefit of May 15, 1828, should receive the amount of his *full pay* in the said line, according to his rank, but not to exceed in any case the pay of a Captain in said line, such full pay to commence on the 4th of March, 1831, and to continue during his natural life.

Persons serving as aforesaid, a term or terms less in

the whole than two years, but not less than *six months,* were authorized to receive for life, each according to his term of service, an amount bearing such proportion to the annuity granted to the same rank for the service of two years, as his term of service did to the term aforesaid, to commence on the 4th of March, 1831.

NOTE.—Under this act, pensioners receiving revolutionary pensions under any preceding act, were not entitled to its benefits unless they first relinquished further claim to such former pension. The officers, non-commissioned officers, seamen, and marines, who served for a like term in the naval service, are entitled to the benefits of this act in the same manner as is provided for the officers and soldiers of the Revolutionary Army.

CHAPTER VI.

Pensioners under the act of June 7, 1832, to receive invalid pensions, if disabled.

On the 19th of February, 1833, it was enacted, that the act of June 7, 1832, should not be construed to embrace invalid pensioners, and that the pensions of invalid soldiers should not be deducted from the amount receivable by them under that act; and by the act of the 2nd of March, 1833, it was declared, that wherever it shall be made to appear that any applicant for a pension entered the Revolutionary Army previous to the 11th of April, 1783, and continued in service until after that period, the time of his service should be computed from the time he then entered the army, until the date af the definitive treaty of peace.

REVOLUTIONARY ARMY PENSIONS.

Widows and Children.

CHAPTER VII.

The Widow or Children to receive the balance due in the case of a deceased Pensioner.

By the act of March 2, 1829, it was provided, that on the death of a revolutionary pensioner, any arrearage of pension due to him shall be paid to his widow, or her attorney; or in case he left no widow, or she be dead, then to the children of the pensioner, or to their guardian or his attorney; and if no child or children, then to the legal representatives of the deceased.

CHAPTER VIII.

Pay allowed from the 4th of March, 1831, *to the Widow or Children of Revolutionary Officers, Soldiers, or Seamen, who died after that time, and before the 7th of June,* 1832.

The 2nd, 4th and 5th sections of the act of July 4, 1836, provided, that in case of the death of any officer, soldier, seaman, or marine, who served in the Revolutionary War in the manner specified by the act of June 7, 1832, since the 6th of March, 1831, and before June 7, 1832, the amount of pension which would have accrued since March 4, 1831, to the time of his death, and been payable to him by the act of June 7, 1832, had he survived the passage thereof, should be paid to his widow, and if he left no widow, to his children, in the manner prescribed by the latter act.

CHAPTER IX.

Widows of Revolutionary Officers and others, allowed Pensions.

The 3rd, 4th, and 5th sections of the act of the 4th of July, 1836, provided, that in case of the death of any person who served in the Revolutionary War in the manner specified by the act of June 7, 1832, leaving a widow whose marriage took place *before the expiration of the last period of his service*, such widow shall be entitled to receive, during the time she may remain unmarried, the annuity or pension which might have been allowed to her husband by virtue of the said act, if living at the time it was passed.

CHAPTER X.

The benefits of the act of July 4, 1836, not to be withheld in certain cases.

On the 3rd of March, 1837, it was enacted that the benefits of the preceding act of July 4, 1836, shall not be withheld from any widow, in consequence of her having married after the decease of her husband, for whose services she may claim a pension under the said act, *provided that she was a widow at the time it was passed.*

The act of March 3, 1837, also declared, that the widow of any person who continued in the service of the United States until November 3, 1783, and was married before that day, and while her husband was in such service, shall be entitled to the benefits of the act of July 4, 1836.

On the 7th of July, 1838, it was resolved, that the death of the husband after July 4, 1836, should not prevent the widow from being pensioned under the act of that date.

CHAPTER XI.

Five years' pension to Widows of Revolutionary Soldiers, if married before 1794.

On July 7, 1838, an act was passed, which declared, that in case of the death of any person who served in the Revolutionary War in the manner specified by the act of June 7, 1832, leaving a widow whose marriage took place *after the expiration of his last period of service* and *before the* 1*st of January,* 1794, such widow shall be entitled to receive for and during the term of *five years,* from the 4th of March, 1836, the pension which might have been allowed to her husband in virtue of the said act of June 7, 1832, if living at the time it was passed, the pension to be discontinued in case of the marriage of said widow.

CHAPTER XII.

Death of the husband after June 7, 1832, *does not prevent the widow from drawing a pension under the act of July* 7, 1838.

On the 16th of August, 1842, a joint resolution was passed, which declared that the benefits of the act of July 7, 1838, shall not be withheld from any widow whose husband died after June 7, 1832, and before the act of July 7, 1838, if otherwise entitled to the same.

CHAPTER XIII.

The marriage of a widow after the death of her husband, for whose service she claims, is no bar to her drawing a pension under the act of July 7, 1838.

On the 23rd of August, 1842, it was enacted, that the marriage of a widow after the death of her husband, for whose service she claims, shall be no bar to her drawing a pension, under the act of July 7, 1838, if she be a widow at the time she makes the application for a pension.

CHAPTER XIV.

One years' pension allowed to certain Widows.

By the act of March 3, 1843, the pensions of widows of revolutionary soldiers entitled to pensions for five years from the 4th of March, 1836, were extended for *one year*, from the 4th of March, 1843.

CHAPTER XV.

Four years additional pension to certain Widows.

On the 17th of June, 1844, the preceding act of March 3, 1843, was revived, and extended for and during the term of *four years*, from and after the 4th of March, 1844, having the same effect as though the said act had had been a grant of pension for *five* years, instead of one year.

CHAPTER XVI.

Widows of Revolutionary Soldiers entitled to a renewal of their pensions for life.

On the 2d of February, 1848, an act was passed, which entitled the aforesaid widows of Revolutionary soldiers, having served in the manner specified by the act of June 7, 1832, to a renewal of their pensions *for life*, or during their widowhood, provided, the marriage took place before January 1, 1794, said renewal to date from March 4, 1848. It was also provided, that such widows as have been admitted by special act of Congress to the benefits of the pension acts of July 7, 1838, and June 17, 1844, shall be admitted to the benefits of this act.

CHAPTER XVII.

The husband's Evidence of Service, if a Pensioner, shall be conclusive proof of the same in his widow's case.

By the act of July 1, 1848, it was provided, that in all cases where a pension may have been granted to any officer or soldier of the Revolution in his life time, the evidence upon which such pension was granted, shall be conclusive of the service of such officer or soldier in the application of any woman who may have been the widow of such officer or soldier; and upon proof that she was married previous to January 1, 1794, and that she is still a widow, entitles her to be placed upon the pension roll, at the same rate that such officer or soldier received during his lifetime.

CHAPTER XVIII.

Widows of Revolutionary Officers and Soldiers may draw pensions, if married before January 1, 1800.

By the act of July 29, 1848, widows of Revolutionary officers and soldiers, mariners, marines, or Indian spies, who served in the continental line, whether in State troops, volunteers, or militia, or in the naval service, are entitled to a pension during such widowhood, of equal amount per annum that their husbands would be entitled to, if living, under existing pension laws, to commence on the 4th of March, 1848; provided, such widow was married previous to the 1st of January, 1800. But no widow receiving a pension at the time of the passage of this act is entitled to a further pension under it.

NOTE.—In all these acts relating to widows, it is declared, that any pledge, mortgage sale, assignment, or transfer of any right, claim, or interest in any way granted by the acts, shall be utterly void and of no effect; nor shall the annuities or pension be liable to attachment, levy, or seizure, by any process of law or equity, but shall inure wholly to the benefit of the pensioner; also, that before a warrant shall be delivered to any person acting for or in behalf of any one entitled to money under their acts, such person shall take and subscribe an oath or affirmation, to be administered by the proper accounting officer, and put on file, that he has no interest in said money, by any pledge, mortgage, transfer, agreement, understanding, or arrangement, and that he does not know or believe that the same has been so disposed of to any other person.

ARMY PENSIONS

FOR SERVICES SUBSEQUENT TO THE REVOLUTION.

CHAPTER XIX.

Pension for Rangers disabled in the service.

The 4th section of the act of January 2, 1812, authorizing the raising of certain companies of Rangers, declared, that the officers, non-commissioned officers, and privates, raised pursuant to that act, should be entitled to the like compensation in cases of disability, by wounds or otherwise, incurred in the service, as the officers and soldiers of the then existing military establishment.

CHAPTER XX.

Pensions to Invalids of the additional forces of 1812.

The fourteenth section of the act of January 11, 1812, "for raising an additional military force" declared, that officers and soldiers raised under that act, should, in case of disability by wounds or otherwise, while in the line of their duty in public service, be placed on the invalid list of the United States. The pension to a commissioned officer not to exceed, for the highest rate of disability, half his monthly pay at the time of his being disabled or wounded, and no officer to receive more than the half pay of a Lieutenant Colonel. The rate of compensation to non-commissioned officers, musicians, and privates, not to exceed *five dollars* per month. All inferior disabilities to entitle the person so disabled, to receive an allowance proportionate to the highest disability.

CHAPTER XXI.

Volunteers disabled in the service to be pensioned.

By the act of February 6, 1812, section 5, *Volunteers* disabled in the service were also pensioned, under the same regulations as the preceding act of January 11, 1812.

CHAPTER XXII.

Provision for those who served in the Wabash Campaign in 1812.

By the act of April 10, 1812, provided, that the officers and soldiers of the volunteers and militia who served in the campaign on the Wabash in 1811 against the Indians, should receive the same compensation as is allowed by law to the militia of the United States, when called into the actual service of the United States. (*See widows'*, Chap. XXVIII.)

CHAPTER XXIII.

Pensions to Invalids of the one years' men.

By the act of January 29, 1813, "for raising an additional military force," section 10 and 11, officers and soldiers raised under that act, if disabled by wounds or otherwise, while in the line of duty in public service, were entitled to be placed on the United States invalid list. The compensation of a commissioned officer for the highest rate of disability, not to exceed half his monthly pay at the time of his being disabled or wounded, and no officer to receive more than the half pay of a Lieutenant Colonel. The compensation of non commissioned officers, musicians, and privates, not to exceed five dollars per month. (*See widows'*, Chap. XXIX.)

CHAPTER XXIV.

Pensions to certain Troops for sea coast defence.

The 2nd section of the act of January 28, 1814, for raising certain troops for sea coast defence, placed the said troops on the same footing in every respect as the other regular troops of the United States.

CHAPTER XXV.

Pensions to Invalids of the Peace Establishment of 1815.

The 7th section of the act of March 3, 1815, placed the several corps authorized by that act on the same footing with regard to wounds and disabilities as is authorized by the act of March 16, 1802.

CHAPTER XXVI.

Pensions to Invalids of Mounted Volunteers for frontier defence.

The 4th section of the act of June 15, 1832, placed the officers and soldiers raised under that act, on the same footing, with regard to wounds and disability, as the soldiers in the United States military establishment.

WIDOWS' PENSIONS

FOR SERVICES OF THEIR HUSBANDS SUBSEQUENT TO THE REVOLUTION.

CHAPTER XXVII.

Widows of Rangers, Sea Fencibles, Militia, and Volunteers killed in the War of 1812 *with Great Britain, allowed pensions.*

The act of April 16, 1816, provides, that any officer or private soldier of the militia, including rangers, sea-fencibles, and volunteers, or any non-commissioned officer, musician, or private, who enlisted for either of the terms, of one year, or eighteen months, or any commissioned officer of the regular army, dieing while in the service of the United States, during the War of 1812 with Great Britain, or in returning to his place of residence after being mustered out of service, or at any time thereafter, in consequence of wounds received in the service, and shall have left a widow, or if no widow, a child or children under sixteen years of age, such widow, or if no widow, such child or children, shall be entitled to receive half the monthly pay to which the deceased was entitled at the time of his death, for and during the term of *five years.* In case of the death or re-marriage of such widow within the said five years, the half pay, for the residue of the time, to go to the child or children.

It provides, also, that officers and private soldiers of the militia as aforesaid, disabled while in the service of the United States, shall be placed on the list of pensioners, in the same manner as the officers and soldiers of the regular army.

The provisions of this act do not extend to any person embraced in the provisions of the act of August 2, 1813, providing for the widows and orphans of militia slain or disabled in the service of the United States.

CHAPTER XXVIII.

Pensions for Widows and Children of Volunteers and Militia who served in the Wabash Campaign in 1811.

The act of April 10, 1812, provided, that officer sand soldiers of the volunteers or militia, who served in the Wabash campaign against the hostile Indians, and who were killed or died of wounds received in said service, leaving a widow, or if no widow, a child or children under sixteen years of age· such widow, or if no widow, such child or children shall be entitled to half the monthly pay to which the deceased was entitled at the time of his death, or receiving the wound of which he died, for, and during the term of five years; and in case of the death or intermarriage of such widow, before the expiration of the term of five years, the half pay for the remainder of the term to go to the child or children, whilst under the age of sixteen.

CHAPTER XXIX.

Five years' half pay to Widows in certain cases.

The act of January 29, 1813, granting pensions to invalids of the one years' men "provided, that in case of the death of any commissioned officer while in the service, by reason of wounds received in the actual service of the United States, his widow, or if no widow, his child or children, should be entitled to receive half his monthly pay for the term of five years. In case of the death or intermarriage of such widow, before the expiration of the term, the residue to go to the child or children.

CHAPTER XXX.

Widows and Orphans of Rangers placed on the same footing with those of Infantry.

By the act of March 3, 1817, sec. 1, 4, the widows and children of soldiers of the militia, the volunteers, soldiers and sea-fencibles, who served during the late war with Great Britain, and for whom half-pay for five years was provided by the act of April 10, 1816, were placed on an equality as to their annual allowance; that is to say, such widows, and in case of no widow, such children, as may be embraced in the before recited act, shall be entitled to receive (as the half pay to which they are entitled) at the rate of forty-eight dollars per annum, and no more; and the widows and children aforesaid, of the officers of the different corps aforesaid, shall be entitled to the half pay of the officers of the infantry; the widows and children of the non-commissioned officers of the rangers shall be placed on the same footing, as to half pay for five years, with the widows and children of the infantry.

CHAPTER XXXI.

The Widow and Children to receive the balance due in the case of a deceased pensioner.

The act of March 2, 1829, authorized the payment to the widow or children, or if no child or children, to the legal representative, the arrears of pension due at the time of his death, in case he died before the certificate of the continuance of his disability, required by the act of March 3, 1819, was obtained, *Provided*, that his last examination was within two years from the time of his death.

CHAPTER XXXII.

Widows and Orphans of Officers and Soldiers of the Militia, Rangers, Sea-Fencibles, and Volunteers, who have died since April 20, 1818, entitled to five years' half pay.

The act of July 4, 1836, sections 1, 4, 5, grants five years' half pay to widows and orphans of officers and soldiers of the militia, rangers, sea-fencibles, and volunteers who have died since April 20, 1818. In case of the intermarriage or death of the widow within the five years, the residue to go to the child or children for the remainder of the term. This act had reference to the Seminole war in Florida, and was, afterwards, re-enacted so as to apply to the Mexican war.

The 2d, 4th, and 5th sections of this act, allow pay to the widows or children of Revolutionary soldiers or seamen, who died after March 4, 1831, and before June 7, 1832.

CHAPTER XXXIII.

Pensions allowed to Widows and Orphans of the Regular Army in certain cases arising in the War with Mexico.

The act of July 21, 1848, declared, that the provisions of the first section of the act of July 4, 1836, granting half pay to widows and orphans of soldiers who died in the military service of the United States, should be applicable to all widows and orphans of soldiers of the United States Army, who were in the Army on March 1, 1846, or subsequently, during the Mexican war. Also, that the widows and orphans of officers or soldiers, whether of the regular army or of volunteers, who have died since April 1, 1846, from wounds received or diseases contracted while in the line of their duty, shall be entitled to the same rate of pensions as is provided in the first section of the act of July 4, 1836,: *Provided*, such death occurred while such soldier was in the service of the United States, and in the line of duty, or while returning to his usual place of residence in the United States, after having received a discharge upon a surgeon's certificate, for disabilities incurred from wounds received, or disease contracted while in the line of duty, or while on his march to join the army in Mexico. This act is not applicable to the widows and orphans of such soldiers who have not served in Mexico, or at posts or stations on the borders of Mexico, except where such soldiers died while on their march to join the army in Mexico.

CHAPTER XXXIV.

Five years' half pay to Widows and Orphans in certain cases.

On the 22d of February, 1849, it was enacted, that the 3rd section of the act of July 21, 1848, shall be so construed as to embrace all widows and orphans of officers, non commissioned officers, musicians and privates, whether of the regular army or of volunteers, who have received an honorable discharge, or who remained to the date of their death in the military service of the United States, and who have died since their return to their usual place of residence, of wounds received, or of diseases contracted while in line of duty.

On the 28th of September, 1850, a joint resolution was passed, which declared, that the provision of the above act shall be construed to embrace the widows and orphans of all persons designated therein, who died while in actual service in the late war with Mexico, or in going to and returning from the same; and also to the widows and orphans of all such persons as, having been honorably discharged, or having resigned, shall have died after the passage of said last mentioned act, of February 22, 1849, or who may hereafter die, of wounds received or from disease contracted while in said service: *Provided*, That the army rolls, showing the death of any of said persons in the army, shall be sufficient evidence to establish that fact.

NAVY PENSIONS.

OFFICERS, SEAMEN, AND MARINES.

CHAPTER XXXV.

Invalids of the Navy allowed pensions.

The act of April 23, 1800, established the Navy pension fund. By this act, every officer, seaman or marine, disabled in the line of his duty, is entitled to a pension for life, according to the nature and degree of his disability, not to exceed one half of his monthly pay.

CHAPTER XXXVI.

Revenue Officers and Seamen allowed pensions in certain cases.

By the act of April 18, 1814, the officers and seamen of the revenue cutters of the United States, who have been or may be wounded or disabled in the discharge of their duty, whilst co-operating with the Navy, by order of the President of the United States, are to be placed on the Navy pension list, at the same rate of pension, and under the same regulations and restrictions, as are provided by law for the officers and seamen of the Navy.

CHAPTER XXXVII.

Naval Engineers, Firemen, and Coal Heavers provided for.

The act of August 11, 1848, declared, that engineers, firemen, and coal heavers in the Navy, shall be entitled to pensions in the same manner as officers, seamen ,and marines. But an engineer, fireman, or coal heaver, is not entitled to any pension for disability incurred prior to August 31, 1842. (*See widows'*, chap. XLIX.)

WIDOWS AND CHILDREN.

CHAPTER XXXVIII.

Five years' pension to Widows and Children of Navy officers killed.

The act of January 20, 1813, granted five years' half pay to the widows and children of naval officers or officers of the marines, who were killed, or who died by reason of wounds received in the service. In case of the death or intermarriage of the widow, before the expiration of the term of five years, the half pay for the remainder of the term to go to the child or children of the deceased officer.

CHAPTER XXXIX.

Five years' pension to Widows and Orphans of pensioners slain in the service.

The act of March 4, 1814, sec. 2, declared, that if any seaman or marine, belonging to the Navy of the United States, shall die; or if any officer, seaman, or marine, belonging to the Navy of the United States, shall have died since the 18th day of June, in the year of our Lord 1812, by reason of a wound received in the line of his duty, leaving a widow, or if no widow, a child or children under sixteen years of age, such widow, or if no widow, such child or children, shall be entitled to receive half the monthly pay to which the deceased was entitled at the time of his death ; which allowance shall continue for the term of five years ; but in case of the death or intermarriage of such widow before the expiration of the said term of five years, the half pay for the remainder of the term shall go to the child or children of the deceased : *Provided*, That such half pay shall cease on the death of such child or children.

CHAPTER XL.

Orphans and Widows of Pensioners slain in armed vessels of the United States, allowed pensions.

The act of March 3, 1817, granted five years' pensions to the widows, and if no widows, to the children under sixteen years of age, of officers, seamen, or marines, who shall die, or shall have died since 18th June, 1812, of disease contracted, or of casualties or injuries received while in the line of duty.

NOTE.—This act was repealed by the act of 22d January, 1824, but the rights which had accrued under it were reserved. It was repealed because so many deaths by yellow fever, in the West Indies, made too heavy a charge upon the fund.

CHAPTER XLI.

Extension of pensions to Widows and Children.

By the act of April 16, 1818, it was declared, that in every case where a person has been put on the pension list, or granted a certificate of pension, by virtue of the first section of an act passed the fourth day of March, in the year eighteen hundred and fourteen, entitled "An act giving pensions to the orphans and widows of persons slain in the public or private armed vessels of the United States," the Secretary of the Navy be, and he is hereby authorized, at the expiration of the term of five years for which any pension certificate shall have been granted as aforesaid, to allow the full monthly pension to which the rank of the deceased would have entitled him for the highest rate of disability; and that such pension shall continue to such person for the further term of five years: *Provided,* That such pension shall cease on the death of such widow, child, or children.

CHAPTER XLII.

Half pay pensions to the Widows and Children of certain officers marines, and seamen, extended.

The act of March 3, 1819, provided, that in all cases where provision has been made, by law, for five years' half pay to the widows and children of officers, seamen, and marines, who were killed in battle, or died of wounds received in battle, or who died in the naval service of the United States, during the late war, the said provision shall be continued for the additional term of five years, to commence at the end of the first term of five years, in each case, respectively, making the provision equal to ten years' half pay; which shall be paid in the manner and out of the fund heretofore designated by law; and the said pensions shall also cease for the reasons mentioned in the said law.

CHAPTER XLIII.

Further extension of the term of half pay to Widows and Children, and repeal of the Act of 3d March, 1817.

The act of January 22, 1824, declared, that in all cases where provision has been made, by law, for five years' half pay to the widows and children of officers, seamen, and marines, who were killed in battle, or who died in the naval service of the United States, during the late war, and also in all cases where provision has been made for extending the term for five years, in addition to the first term of five years, the said provision shall be further extended for an additional term of five years, to commence at the end of the second term of five years, in each case, respectively, making the provision equal to fifteen years' half pay, which shall be paid out of the fund heretofore provided by law; and the said pension shall cease, for the causes mentioned in the laws providing the same, respectively. From and after the passing this act, the act entitled "An act to amend and explain an act giving pensions to the orphans and widows of persons slain in the public or private armed vessels of the United States," passed March the third, one thousand eight hundred and seventeen, is hereby repealed: *Provided, however,* that nothing in this act contained shall be construed to prevent the payment of any pension already granted, until the full expiration of the period thereof; nor to effect or impair the rights of any person or persons which may have occurred during the existence of the act hereby repealed, as aforesaid.

CHAPTER XLIV.

Extending the term of certain Pensions.

By the act of May 23, 1828, section 1, naval pensions

to widows and orphans of officers and seamen killed in the war of 1812, a fourth term of five years, half pay was granted, making the pensions equal to twenty years half pay.

CHAPTER XLV.

Further extension of Pensions heretofore granted.

The act of June 28, 1832, made a provision for a fifth term of five years, half pay, as far as respects widows only.

CHAPTER XLVI.

Further extension of Naval Pensions.

The act of June 30, 1834, extended for a still further period of five years, the half pay pensions of widows; and also extended it to the widows of naval officers and seamen who died in the naval service since the 1st of January, 1824, by means of disease contracted or injuries received while in the service; the pension to commence from the passage of this act, viz: June 30, 1834.

CHAPTER XLVII.

Pensions to Widows and Children of those who have died in the Naval service.

The act of 3d March, 1837, granted pensions to the widows, and if no widows, to the children under twenty one years of age, of all officers seamen and marines "who have died, or may hereafter die, in the naval service. It provided, that pensions already granted, or to be granted to invalids, shall be paid from the time when they were disabled; and it repeals all acts inconsistent with itself."

CHAPTER XLVIII.

Navy pensions renewed to certain Widows for five years.

The act of March 3, 1845, extended for a further term of five years, the half pay pensions of widows of officers or seamen, to commence from the day on which the last term of five years terminated: *Provided*, said widows remained unmarried.

CHAPTER XLIX.

Naval pensions of certain Widows and Orphans renewed

The act of August 11, 1848, declared, that the widows and children, at the time of receiving pensions under any act of Congress passed prior to August 1, 1841, (except the law of March 3, 1837), and those widows and children who had received pensions at any time within five years prior to August 11, 1848, should continue to receive the same amount as they had received under any special act, from the time such special act expired, *Provided*, such act ceased on or after September 1, 1845, or may hereafter terminate, said renewed pensions to be paid so long as the widows remained unmarried; in case of their death, the pension to go to the children of the deceased parties until they arrive respectively at the age of sixteen. It was also declared, that the act of April 30, 1844, shall not be so construed as to exclude officers, seamen, or marines, from their pensions when disabled, for sea service: *Provided*, that the whole amount received by the pensioner, including pay for his service, and pension, shall not exceed his lowest duty pay; that the orphan child or children of the deceased parties shall have a pension, in case the widow has died after drawing a five years' pension, to commence at the time when the widow dies, and to continue until the child or children shall attain the age of sixteen; and that any casualty, by which an officer, seaman, or marine, has lost, or may lose his life while in the line of his duty, shall be considered sufficient to entitle the widow, child, or children, to all the benefits of this act.

The second section of the act, (of August 11, 1848) enacted, that engineers, firemen, and coal-heavers in the Navy, shall be entitled to pensions in the same manner as officers, seaman, and marines, and the widows of engineers, coal-heavers, and firemen, in the same manner as the widows of officers, seamen and marines, *Provided,* that the pension of a chief engineer shall be the same as that of a lieutenant of the Navy, and a pension of the widow of a chief engineer the same as that of a widow of a lieutenant of the Navy; the pension of a first assistant engineer, the same as that of a lieutenant of marines; and the pension of the widow of a first assistant engineer, the same as that of a widow of a lieutenant of marines; the pension of a second or third assistant engineer the same as that of a pensioned officer; and the pension of a widow of a second or third assistant engineer, the same as that of the widow of a pensioned officer; the pension of a fireman or coal-heaver, the same as that of a seaman; the pension of the widow of a fireman or coal-heaver, the same as that of the widow of a seaman, *Provided further,* that an engineer, fireman or coal-heaver, shall not be entitled to any pension by reason of a disability incurred prior to August 31, 1842, nor shall the widow of an engineer, fireman, or coal-heaver, be entitled to any pension by reason of the death of her husband, if his death was prior to the said date.

The third section enacts, that the amount of pension in every case arising under this law, shall not exceed the half pay of the deceased officer, seaman, or marine, as it existed in January, 1835, or such rate of pension as is allowed by this act.

CHAPTER L.

Persons not entitled to Pensions while in service, except in certain cases.

The act of April 30, 1844, declared, that no person in the Army, Navy, Marine Corps, shall be allowed to draw both a pension as an invalid, and the pay or rank of his station in the service, unless the alledged disability for which the pension was granted, be such as to have occasioned his employment in a lower grade, or in some civil branch of the service.

CHAPTER LI.

Widows and husbands shall not draw Pensions lor the same period.

The act of April 30, 1844, also declared, that no pension shall be hereafter granted to a widow for the same time that her husband received one.

VIRGINIA PENSIONS.

CHAPTER L.

Half pay to Officers of the Virginia Troops and Navy.

By the act of the 5th of July, 1832, it was enacted, that the proper accounting officers of the Treasury are required to liquidate and pay the accounts of the Commonwealth of Virginia against the United States, for payments to the officers commanding in the Virginia line in the war of the Revolution, on account of half pay for life promised the officers aforesaid by that Commonwealth, the sum of one hundred and thirty-nine thousand five hundred and forty-three dollars and sixty-six cents. The Secretary of the Treasury be, and he is hereby, required and directed to pay to the State of Virginia, the amount of the judgments which have been rendered against the said State for and on account of the promise contained in an act passed by the General Assembly of the State of Virginia, in the month of May anno Domini one thousand seven hundred and seventy-nine, and in favor of the officers or representatives of officers of the regiments and corps hereinafter recited, and not exceeding, in the whole, the sum of two hundred and forty-one thousand three hundred and forty-five dollars, to wit:

1st. To the officers, or their legal representatives, of the regiment commanded by the late Colonel George Gibson, the amount of the judgments which they have obtained, and which are now unsatisfied.

2nd. To the officers, or their legal representatives, of the regiment denominated the second State regiment, commanded at times by Colonels Brent and Dabney, the amount of the judgments which they have obtained, and which are now unsatisfied.

3rd. To the officers, or their legal representatives, of the regiments of Colonels Clark and Crockett, and Captain Rogers's troop of cavalry, who were employed in the Illinois service, the amount of the judgments which they have obtained, and which are now unsatisfied.

4th. To the officers, or their legal representatives, serving in the regiment of State artillery commanded by the late Colonel Marshall, and those serving in the State garrison regiment commanded by Colonel Muter, and serving in the State cavalry commanded by Major Nelson, the amount of the judgments which they have obtained, and which are now unsatisfied.

5th. To the officers, or their legal representatives, who served in the navy of Virginia during the war of the Revolution, the amount of the judgments which they have obtained, and which are now unsatisfied.

The Secretary of the Treasury be, and he is hereby, directed and required to adjust and settle those claims for half pay of the officers of the aforesaid regiments and corps, which have not been paid or prosecuted to judgment against the State of Virginia, and for which said State would be bound, on the principles of the half pay cases already decided in the supreme court of appeals of said State ; which several sums of money herein directed to be settled or paid, shall be paid out of any money in the treasury not otherwise appropriated by law.

EXECUTIVE REGULATIONS AND RULES OF EVIDENCE.

Rules of Evidence relating to Invalid Pensions.

The following rules of evidence are applicable to the act of the 25th of April, 1808, chapter 1, page 9.

" In substantiating the claim of any soldier, of whatever grade, who has been wounded or disabled since the Revolutionary War, while in the line of his duty in the actual service of the United States, whether belonging to the regular army, the militia, or to any volunteer corps called into the service of the United States, the following rules and regulations are to be complied with.

All evidence shall be taken on oath or affirmation, before the Judge of the District, or one of the Judges of the State or Territory (Act April 18, 1814,) in which such claimant resides, or before some person specially authorized by commission from said judge. Decisive disability, the effect of a known wound or injury received while in the actual service and line of duty, must be proved by the affidavit of the commanding officer of the regiment, corps, company, ship, vessel, or craft, in which such claimant served, or of two other credible witnesses to the same effect, setting forth the time when, and place where, such known wound or injury was received, and particularly describing the same. The nature of such disability, and in what degree it prevents the claimant from obtaining his subsistence, must be proved by the affidavit of some reputable physician or surgeon, stating his opinion, either from his own knowledge and acquaintance with the claimant, or from an examination of such claimant, on oath or affirmation, which, when necessary for that purpose, shall be administered to said claimant by said judge or commissioner; and the said physician or surgeon, in his affidavit, shall particularly describe the wound or injury from whence the disability appears to be derived. Every claimant must prove, by at least one credible witness, that he continued in service during the whole time for which he was detached, or for which he engaged, unless he was discharged, or left the service in consequence of some derangement of the army, or in consequence of his disability resigned his commission, or was, after his disability, in captivity or on parole; and, in the same manner, must prove his mode of life and employment since he left the service and the place or places where he has since resided, and his place of residence at the time of taking such testimony. Every claimant shall, by his affidavit, give satisfactory reasons why he did not make application for a pension before, and that he is not on the pension list of any State; and the judge or commissioner shall certify, in writing, his opinion of the credibility of the witnesses whose affidavits he shall take, in all those cases where, by this act, it is said the proof shall be made by a credible witness or witnesses; and, also, that the examining physician or surgeon is reputable in his profession. The said judge of the district, or person by him commissioned as aforesaid, shall transmit a list of such claims, accompanied by the evidence, affidavits, certificates, and proceedings had thereon, in pursuance of this act, noting particularly the day on which the testimony was closed before him, to the Secretary for the Department of War, &c. And it shall be the duty of the judge or commissioner aforesaid to permit each claimant to take a transcript of the evidence and proceedings had respecting his claim, it he shall desire it, and to certify the same to be correct. An increase of pension may be allowed to persons already placed upon the pension-list of the United States, for disabilities caused by known wounds received during the revolutionary war, in all cases where justice shall require the same: *Provided*, That the increase, when added to the pension formerly received, shall in no case exceed a full pension. Every invalid making application for this purpose, shall be examined by two reputable physicians or surgeons, to be authorized by commission from the judge of the district where such invalid resides, who shall report in writing, on oath or affirmation, their opiaion of the nature of the applicant's disability, and in what degree it prevents him from obtaining a subsistence by manual labor; which report shall be transmitted by said physicians or surgeons to the Secretary for the Department of War."

Evidence when the Discharge or Surgeon's Certificate has been lost or destroyed.

The following evidence will be required in all militia cases, and cases of the regular army of every grade where the discharge and surgeon's certificate have been lost or destroyed, or where none has been given, to enable the Secretary of War to grant pensions, viz:

"In cases where the regular discharge and surgeon's certificate for disability cannot be had, the applicant for a pension, whether he has been a soldier of the regular army, or a militiaman in the service of the United States, must produce the sworn certificate of his captain, or other officer, under whom he served, stating distinctly the time and place of his having been wounded, or otherwise disabled, and that the same wounds or disabilities arose while in the service of the United States, and in the line of his duty; with the affidavit of one or more surgeons, or physicians, whether of the army or citizens, accurately describing the wound, and stating the degree of disability to which the soldier may be entitled under it. These documents to be sworn to before a judge of the United States Court, or some judge or justice of the peace; and if a State judge, or justice of the peace, then under the seal of the clerk of the county in which such judge or justice may reside; and the name of the paymaster who last paid the soldier, as belonging to the service of the United States, to be in every instance furnished by the applicant, in order to a due examination of the muster-rolls."

An applicant for a pension is not entitled thereto, unless he has been mustered in the United States' service, and joined his regiment or corps.—(*Letter of Secretary* CALHOUN *to Hon.* JOHN HOLMES, *Alfred, Maine, Oct.* 4, 1821.)

Proof of identity is required in cases where the pension has not been claimed for one year or more. The proof will consist of the certificate of a magistrate in the county in which the pensioner resides, setting forth, either that he knows the applicant to be the identical pensioner named in the original pension certificate, which he must exhibit to the magistrate, or that it has been satisfactorily proven before him that he is such pensioner; the signature of the magistrate to be certified under the seal of the court of the county.—(*Letter of Secretary* CALHOUN *to* JAMES L. EDWARDS, *the Commissioner of Pensions, June,* 1824.)

Where the rolls do not show the disability of an applicant, the pension will not be granted without explanation.—(*Letter of Secretary* CALHOUN *to Hon.* PETER

LITTLE, *Chairman of the Committee on Pensions, January* 10, 1825.)

The rule of April 11, 1831, which directs, that no application for an increase of pension, except at the biennial examination, is rescinded. All applications for increase will, however, be made as heretofore, through the Pension Agents, in order that the agents may certify as to the character of the surgeons; except in cases only where the surgeons are known at the department, or where the examinations are made by surgeons of the Army.—(*Secretary* CASS, *Nov.* 17, 1831.)

On January 30, 1832, Secretary CASS revived the rule which declares, that the evidence is perfect when no objection whatever exists to the admission of a claim. The effect of this was to cause a pension to commence at the date of the last certificate which authenticates the papers.

Rules of Evidence under the Act of June 7, 1832, *which makes provision for all who served six months during the Revolution.* (*See chap. V, page* 12.)

The following regulations were, in June 27, 1832, adopted by the Secretary of War for carrying into effect the act of June 7, 1832, supplementary to the act for the relief of the surviving officers and soldiers of the Revolution.

This law has been construed to extend as well to the line as to every branch of the staff of the army, and to include, under the terms "continental line," "State troops," "militia," and "volunteers," all persons enlisted, dranghted, or who volunteered, and who were bound to milita-y service, but not those who were occasionally employed with the army upon civil contracts, such as clerks to commissaries and to storekeepers, &c., teamsters, boatmen, &c.

Four general classes of cases are embraced in this law—

1. The regular troops.
2. The State troops, militia, and volunteers.
3. Persons employed in the naval service.
4. Indian spies.

1. As rolls of the regular troops in the Revolutionary war exist in this department, all persons claiming the benefit of this law, as officers, non-commissioned officers, musicians, or privates, will, in the first instance, make application by transmitting the following declaration, which will be made before a court of record of the country where such applicant resides. And every court of record having, by law, a seal and clerk, is considered a court of record. (*See Forms.*)

Every applicant will produce the best proof in his power. This is the original discharge or commission; but if neither of these can be obtained, the party will so state under oath; and will then procure, if possible, the testimony of at least one credible witness; stating. in detail, his personal knowledge of the services of the applicant, and such circumstances connected therewith as may have a tendency to throw light upon the transaction.

If such surviving witness cannot be found, the applicant will so state in his declaration; (*l*) and he will also, whether he produce such evidence or not, proceed to relate all the material facts which can be useful in the investigation of his claim, and in the comparison of his narrative with the events of the period of his alleged service, as they are known at the department. A very full account of the services of each person will be indispensable to a favorable action upon his case. The facts stated will afford one of the principal means of corroborating the declaration of the applicant, if true, or of detecting the imposition, if one be attempted; and unless, therefore, these are amply and clearly set forth, no favorable decision can be expected. All applicants will appear before some court of record in the county in which they reside, and there subscribe and be sworn to one of the declarations above provided, according to the nature of his case.

The court will propound the following interrogatories (*m*) to all applicants for a pension, on account of service in the militia, State troops, or volunteers, except the militia of New Hampshire and the State troops of Virginia:

1. Where, and in what year, were you born?
2. Have you any record of your age? And, if so, where is it?
3. Where were you living when called into service; where have you lived since the revolutionary war; and where do you now live?
4. How were you called into service; were you draughted, did you volunteer, or were you a substitute; and, if a substitute, for whom?
5. State the names of some of the regular officers who were with the troops where you served; such continental and militia regiments as you can recollect; and the general circumstances of your service?
6. *To a soldier.*—Did you ever receive a discharge from the service; and if so, by whom was it given; and what has become of it?

To an officer.—Did you ever receive a commission; and, if so, by whom was it signed; and what has become of it?

7. State the names of persons to whom you are known in your present neighborhood, and who can testify as to your character for veracity, and their belief of your services as a soldier of the Revolution.

The court will see that the answers to these questions are embodied in the declaration, and they are requested to annex their opinions of the truth of the statement of the applicant.

The applicant will further produce in court, if the same can be done, in the opinion of the court. without too much expense and inconvenience to him, two respectable persons, (one of whom should be the nearest clergyman, if one lives in the immediate vicinity of such applicant,) who can testify, from their acquaintance with him, that they believe he is of the age he represents, and that he is reputed and believed in the neighborhood to have been a revolutionary soldier, and that they concur in that opinion. If one of these persons is a clergyman, the court will so certify; and they will also certify to the character and standing of other persons giving such certificates.

The traditionary evidence of service is deemed very important (*k*) in the absence of any direct proof, except the declaration of the party; and the courts are requested to be very particular in the inquiry whether the belief is general, and whether any doubts have ever existed upon the subject. To require from the applicants positive proof service from a contemporary survivor, would, after the lapse of so many years, be to deprive many of them of the benefit of the law; and, as no presumption is raised against the militia by the existence of rolls in the department, there is no good reason why this requisition should be extended to them. On the other hand, to receive the declaration of the parties as a sufficient ground for placing them upon the pension roll, without corroborating circumstances, would be to open the treasury to great frauds. A just medium seems to present the best rule for carrying into effect the objects of Congress.

If the two persons whose certificates are required cannot be produced in court without too much inconvenience and expense to the applicant, then the statement of the facts and opinions above mentioned will be made under oath, before some judge or justice of the peace; and the certificate of the court to the situation and credibility of the persons making the statement will be given.

Applicants unable to appear in court by reason of bodily infirmity, may make the declaration before required, and submit to the examination before a judge or justice of a court of record of the proper county, and the judge or justtce will execute the duties which the court is herein requested to perform, and will also certify that the applicant cannot, from bodily infirmity, attend the court.

Whenever any official act is required to be done by a judge or justice of a court of record, or by a justice of the peace, the certificate of the Secretary of State or Territory, or of the proper clerk of the court or county, under his seal of office, will be annexed, stating that such person is a judge or justice of a court of record, or a justice of the peace, and that the signature annexed is his genuine signature.

3. Persons serving in the marine forces.
4. Indian spies.

Each of these two latter classes of cases will produce proof, as nearly as may be conformably to the preceding regulations, and authenticated in a similar manner, with such variations as the different nature of the service may require. No payments can be made on account of the services of any person who may have died before the taking effect of the act of June 7 1832; and, in case of death subsequent thereto, and before the declaration herein required is made, the parties interested will transmit such evidence as they can procure, taken and authenticated before a court of record, showing the services of the deceased, the period of his death, the opiniou of the neighborhood respecting such services, the title of the claimant, ank the opinion of the court upon the whole matter."

☞ For notes see Declaration, page 55.

By the resolution of Congress of the 14th July, 1832, the time of imprisonment as a prisoner of war shall be taken and computed as a part of the period of service, in the execution of the act of June 7, 1832.

A Commission not indispensable in all cases to entitle an Officer to a pension.

Service in a military office, even though the commission may not be issued, or may not date back to the commencement of the service, entitles the person to a pension for such service, (*Letter of Secretary* CASS *to* J. L. EDWARDS, *January* 15, 1833.

Regulations respecting the Payment of Arrears to the Children of deceased pensioners.

On November 9, 1833, Secretary Cass ruled that "in a case where the residence of all the children of a deceased pensioner cannot be ascertained, those who are known to be living must prove their relationship to the deceased before a court of record; they must show that the pensioner left no widow; that the children, who are in parts unknown have not been heard of for at least one full year, and that exertions have been made, without success, to ascertain their residence. Their names must be given. The court must give a certificate containing the facts, and the clerk of the court must sign the same, and annex thereto his seal of office. In such a case, the amount due will be paid to those who are known to be living; and all that is due must be paid at one time.

In a case where there is no widow, and the children who survive reside at a considerable distance from each other, and it is difficult or impractable to obtain information or powers of attorney from those who live remote from the pension agency, the amount due to each child may be paid, upon proper vouchers when demanded, without requiring all the children to make application at the same time.

Evidence of a Commission necessary in certain cases.

WAR DEPARTMENT, *February* 21*st*, 1833.

Claims are frequently presented under the act of January 7, 1832, of persons who allege that they acted as officers without receiving commissions. Such applications should be received with caution, and examined with special reference to the peculiar circumstances of each case. A commission is not in every case indispensably necessary to invest a person with rank or command, or to entitle him to the emoluments of the office which he fills; but some act or instrument of writing tantamount to a commission, or promise of a commission, is deemed essential. It must in all cases be clearly shown that the person who claims as an officer, and never held a commission as such, was prevented from receiving one in consequence of peculiar circumstances over which he had no control. The mere asseveration of a person as to his having performed the duty incumbent on an officer of a certain grade, does not entitle him to the pension due to an officer of that grade.

LEWIS CASS.

November 29, 1833, it was ruled by Secretary CASS, that members of Congress may certify to the character of a surgeon, to be received in a case where the pensioner cannot conveniently obtain the certificate of the agent for paying pensions.

On June 17, 1834, Secretary CASS decided, that "the rule of December 23, 1817, which requires the testimony of a commissioned officer to show the origin and nature of the corporal disability of an applicant for a pension, may be dispensed with in a case where it is clearly shown that such evidence cannot be obtained, and where other satisfactory proof of disability can be obtained. In such a case, the following rules of evidence will be adhered to:

1. The applicant must make a declaration setting forth all the material facts in the case, and the surgeons must testify as the rule of December 23, 1817, directs.

2. He must prove, by persons of known respectability, that the officers mentioned by the claimant in his deposition are dead, or removed to such a distance as to render it impracticable to obtain their affidavits. The person or persons who may give such evidence must state particularly all the knowledge they may possess in relation to the death or removal of such officers.

3. In such a case as that mentioned in rule No. 2, the applicant must

produce the testimony of at least two creditable witnesses, whose good character must be vouched for by some one known to this department. The witnesses must give a minute narrative of all the facts in relation to the matter, and it must be shown conclusively, by their testimony, that the disability of the claimant is to be ascribed solely to injury sustained while the claimant was in the discharge of military duty in the service of the United States. The witnesses must show how they acquired a knowledge of the facts set forth, and state in what capacity or grade they served.

The affidavits must be authenticated in the same manner prescribed by the rule of December 23, 1817.

A person discharged as a Minor not deprived of his right to a pension.

FEBRUARY 10, 1836.

If a person enlists in the service, and, while there, is disabled, and entitled under existing laws to a pension, and subsequently discharged before the expiration of his term, as a minor, I think he does not lose his claim to a pension. LEWIS CASS.

Declarations may be made by a relative of a Claimant in case of insanity.

On consultation with the Attorney General he is of opinion, that *in all cases* of insanity or of mental infirmity destroying the faculties, the *statement* of the nearest relatives of a person claiming a pension may be received under oath, recapitulating his own account of his *services* as given prior to such incapacity; and that, if such statement would have been *sufficient* to warrant the pension, if made by the party himself, it shall be deemed sufficient in those cases.

Let this be the rule. LEWIS CASS.

Rules of evidence in Widows and Orphans' claims.

In order to carry into effect the Act of the 4th of July, 1836, granting half pay to widows and orphans in certain cases, (see chapter IX,) the following rules have been prescribed.

1. Applicants under the first section of the act must produce the best proof the nature of the case will allow as to the service of the deceased officer or soldier; the time when he died, and the complaint of which he died, and the supposed cause of his disease. It must be clearly shown in what company, and regiment or corps, he served, and the grade he held. Such proof must be had, either from the records of the War Department, the muster-rolls, the testimony of commissioned officers, or the affidavits of persons of known respectability. From similar sources evidence must be derived as to the period and cause of the death of the officer or soldier.

2. The legality of the marriage, the name of the widow, with those of her children who may have been under sixteen years of age at the time of the father's decease, with the State or Territory and county in which she and they reside, should be established. The legality of the marriage may be ascertained by the certificate of the clergyman who joined them in wedlock, or the testimony of respectable persons having knowledge of the fact. The age and number of children may be ascertained by the deposition of the mother, accompanied by the testimony of respectable persons having knowledge of them, or by transcripts from the parish registers, duly authenticated. The widow, at the time of allowing the half pay, or placing her on the list for it, must show that she has not again married, and must, moreover, repeat this at the time of receiving each and every payment thereof; because, in case of her marrying again, the half pay to her ceases, and the half pay for the remainder of the time shall go to the child or children of the decedent. This may be done by the affidavits of respectable persons having knowledge of the case.

3. In cases where there are children and no widow, their guardian will of course act for them, establish their claims as prescribed in the foregoing resolutions, and receive their stipends for them.

4. Applicants under the second section of the law will make a declaration before a court of record, setting forth, according to the best of her or their knowledge or belief, the names and rank of the field and company officers, the day (if possible) and the month and year when the claimant's husband or father (as the case may be) entered the service, and the time when he left the same; and if under more than one engagement, the claimant must specify the particular periods, and the rank and names of the officers under whom the service was performed; the town or county and State in which the claimant's husband or father resided when he entered the service—whether he was draughted, was a volunteer or substitute; the battles, if any, in which he was engaged; the country through which he marched, with such further particulars as may be useful in the investigation of the claim; and, also, if the fact be so, that the claimant has no documentary evidence in support of the claim.

5. The same description of proof as to the relationship of the claimant to the deceased officer or soldier will be required as the rule under the first section points out.

6. Claimants under the third section of the law must not only produce such proof as the foregoing regulations direct in relation to widows' claims, but they must, in all cases, as an indispensable requisite, show when they were legally married to the deceased officer or soldier on account of whose services the claim is presented, and that the marriage took place before the last term of service of the husband expired. They must also prove that they were never afterwards married.

7. In a case where the service of the deceased officer or soldier is clearly proved by record or documentary evidence, or the affidavit of a commissioned officer, showing the grade and length of service of the deceased, the particulars in relation to the service are not required to be set forth in the claimant's declaration, except so far as to show that the claimant or claimants is or are the widow or children of the deceased.

8. The claimant must, in every case where there is no record or documentary proof of the revolutionary service of the deceased officer or sol-

dier, produce the testimony of at least one credible witness. Traditionary evidence will be deemed useful in every such case.

9. Applicants unable to appear in court, by reason of bodily infirmity, may make the declaration before required before a judge or justice of a court of record of the county in which the applicant resides; and the judge or justice will certify that the applicant cannot, from bodily infirmity, attend the court.

10. Whenever any official act is required to be done by a judge or justice of a court of record, or by a justice of the peace, the certificate of the Secretary of State or of the Territory, or of the proper clerk of the court or county, under his seal of office, will be annexed, stating that such a person is a judge or justice of a court of record, or a justice of the peace, and that the signature annexed is his genuine signature.

11. The widows of those who served in the navy, or as Indian spies, will produce proof, as nearly as may be, conformably to the preceding regulations, and authenticated in a similar manner, with such variations as the different nature of the service may require.

12. The form prescribed for claimants under the third section of the act will be observed by every other description of claimants, so far as the same may be applicable to their cases. The judge or justice who may administer an oath must, in every instance, certify to the credibility of the affiant.

13. In every case in which the deceased officer or soldier was a pensioner, the fact should be so stated; and the deceased pensioner so described as to enable the department to refer immediately to the evidence upon which he was pensioned, and thus facilitate the investigation of the claim of his widow or children.

JAMES L. EDWARDS,
Commissioner of Pensions.

Pension of a Husband not to be deducted in certain cases.

On the 24th of July, 1837, J. L. EDWARDS, the Commissioner of Pensions, made the following inquiry in reference to the case of Catherine Oakley.

Can the pension paid to William Oakley, during the time he was husband to Catharine Oakley, be deducted from the amount due to her, under the act of July 4, 1836, on account of the revolutionary services of William Douglass, to whom she was married during said service?

I have the honor to be, very respectfully, your obedient servant,

J. L. EDWARDS.

Hon. JOEL R. POINSETT,
Secretary of War.

REPLY.—The pension paid to Oakley during the period he was husband of Catharine, widow of Douglass, ought not to be deducted from the pension due her on account of the services of her former husband.

J. R. P.

Rules of Evidence under the Act of 7th July, 1838, granting half pay and pensions to certain widows, if married prior to January 1st, 1794. (*See chap.* XI.)

1. Applicants must produce the best proof the nature of the case will allow as to the service of the deceased officer or soldier, and the time, when he died. It must be clearly shown in what troop or company, and regiment or corps, he served, and the grade he held. Proof as to service must be had, either from the records of the War Department, the muster-rolls, the testimony of commissioned officers, or the affidavits of persons of known respectability. Every applicant will make a declaration according to the subjoined form, before a court (*a*) of record, setting forth, according to the best of her knowledge or belief, the name and rank of the person on account of whose service the claim is presented; the day, month, and year, (if possible,) when he entered the service, and the time when he left the same; and, if under more than one engagement, the claimant must specify the particular periods, and the rank and name of the officers under whom the service was performed; the town or county, and State, in which he resided when he entered the service; whether he was draughted, was a volnnteer, or a substitute; the battles, if any, in which he was engaged; the country through which he marched, with such further particulars as may be useful in the investigation of the claim; and also, if the fact be so, that the claimant has no documentary evidence in support of the claim. From the best sources of information evidence must be derived as to the period of the death (*b*) of the officer or soldier.

2. The legality of the marriage, and the time when it took place, must be clearly established; and it must also be shown that the widow was never afterwards married. Record proof, as to the marriage, is always required, whenever it can be obtained. In a case where the town, county, parish, church, or family records afford no proof as to the period when the marriage took place, the fact must be established by the testimony of one or more respectable persons, whose credibility must be certified by the officer who may administer the oath. And, in order to prevent any mistake or improper use that may be made of the affidavit of an officer who may have the custody of records, from which he may make transcripts of the record in relation to a marriage, the officer who may give his affidavit will, instead of copying the figures contained in the record, certify "that it is a true copy of the record, with the exception of the date, which is expressed on the record in fair legible figures, as follows :" [Here copy the day, month, and year, in letters and figures, in exact conformity with the original. Then let him add the following words:]

"I, A B, above named, depose and say, that I hold the office of

EXPLANATORY NOTES

(*a*) The declaration of the widow who claims must be made in all cases, in open court, unless she is prevented, from bodily infirmity, from appearing before the court.

(*b*) It must, in all cases, be shown in what year the husband died. The testimony on this point must be positive, and the language must be free from all ambiguity.

in the county, town, and State aforesaid, and that the above is a true extract from the records of said , with the exception above named, as certified by me.

A B, *Clerk ef the*
(or rector, or pastor, as the case may be)

Sworn before me, C D, *Justice of the Peace.'*

And then will follow the certificate of the proper officer, under his seal of office, as to the official character and signature of the magistrate who may administer the oath. Where no record proof exists, other than the family record, the original record must be produced and sworn to by the person in whose possession it has been kept. (*c*.)

3. In a case where the service of the deceased officer or soldier is clearly proved by record or documentary evidence, or the affidavit of a commissioned officer, showing the grade and length of service of the deceased, the particulars in relation to the service are not required to be set forth in the claimant's declaration; but she must swear, in positive terms, that she is the widow of the person whose service is thus proved. And no claim whatever can be sustained without positive proof of service.

4. In every case in which the deceased officer or soldier was a pensioner, the fact should be so stated, and the deceased pensioner so described as to enable the Department to refer immediately to the evidence upon which he was pensioned, and thus facilitate the investigation of the claim of the widow.

5. Applicants unable to appear in court, by reason of bodily infirmity, may make the declaration before required before a judge or justice (*d*) of a court of record in the county in which the applicant resides, and the judge or justice will certify that the applicant cannot, from bodily infirmity, attend the court.

6. Whenever any official act is required to be done by a judge or justice of a court of record, or by a justice of the peace, the certificate of the Secretary of State or of the Territory, or of the proper officer or clerk of the court or county, under his seal of office, will be annexed, stating that such a person is a judge, or a justice of a court of record, or a justice of the peace, and that the signature annexed is his genuine signature.

7. The widows of those who served in the navy, or as Indian spies will produce proof, as nearly as may be, conformably to the preceding regulations, and authenticated in a similar manner, with such variations as the different nature of the service may require.

J. L. EDWARDS,
Commissioner of Pensions.

(*c*) The family record must be sent to the Pension Office, if there be no other record, accompanied by the oath of the person in whose possession it has been kept. The person who may swear to the genuineness of the record should give the name of the person in whose handwriting the record was made.

(*d*) A declaration before a justice of the peace cannot be admitted as evidence.

Certificate of United States judge as to the character of a surgeon.

WAR DEPARTMENT, *December* 4, 1838.

The rule of November 17, 1831, is hereby so amended as to allow the certificate of a judge of any of the United States courts, as to the character of a surgeon or physician, to be received in a case where the pensioner cannot conveniently obtain the certificate of the agent for paying pensioners.

J. R. POINSETT,
Secretary of War.

In March, 1839, Secretary WOODBURY decided, that children of soldiers, or of their widows, may draw what was due to their parents when they died, although the proof might not have been perfected at their death.

On January 5, 1840, Secretary POINSETT decided, that the children of the widow, after her death, and not an executor, are entitled to the amount due her.

In August 31, 1840, Secretary POINSETT decided, that the failure of a soldier to return to duty after captivity, is to be viewed as desertion, and is not entitled to a pension.

On November 17, 1842, Secretary SPENCER decided, that second marriage is no bar to a claim under the act of July 7, 1838, if the claimant be a widow at the time of her application.

By a decision of Secretary SPENCER, February 6, 1843, the benefit of the joint resolution of August 16, 1842, was ruled to extend to those widows only who were then living.

On November 14, 1843, Secretary PORTER decided, that surgeons, under the act of 7th of June, 1832, should be entitled to the highest rate of pension, according to the length of service.

Secretary PORTER also made the following decisions, viz:

1. Desertion forfeits all right to a pension. (*June* 27, 1843.)

2. A widow may receive a pension for the service of two husbands, but is not entitled to two pensions for the same term. (*Dec.* 13, 1843.)

3. Under the act of 15 May, 1828, surgeons are entitled to only Infantry Captain's pay.

In May, 1844, Secretary WILKINS made the following decisions relative to the act of 30th April, 1844.

1. If the husband was a pensioner, and died at any time between the 4th March, 1836, and the 4th of March, 1841, the widow is entitled to that portion of the five years' pension which accrued between the day of his death, when his pension ceased, and the 4th of March, 1841.

2. If the husband died at any time between the 4th of March, 1841, and the 3d of March, 1843, the widow is entitled to the benefit of the law of March 3, 1843, which allows one year's pension to all those widows who were entitled to the benefits of the acts of July 7, 1838, and August 23d, 1842?

3. The act of April, 1844, operates on all claims filed in the office prior to the passage of the act, as well as to all subsequent cases.

The following decisions were also made by Secretary WILKINS, viz:

1. The rank of an officer is dependent on his commission, and half pay is dependent on his rank. (*June* 15, 1844.)

2. The act of June 17, 1844, is a continuation of the act of March 3, 1843. (*June* 20, 1844.)

3. A pensioner is not excluded from half pay under the act of July 5, 1832. (*July* 6, 1844.)

4. The pensions due to a widow can, in no case, go to the executor or administrator, if there be a child or children. (*July* 18, 1844.)

Rules respecting the amputation of a Pensioner's limb.

WAR DEPARTMENT, *August* 28, 1845.

The practice of the department to commence the increase of an invalid pension on the day when proof is made of an increase of disability, is very proper, and is in conformity with the principles laid down in the invalid pension laws; and the reason of the law is, that it is presumed in all cases that the claimant will perfect his proof as soon as his disability is so increased as to render it proper to ask for an augmentation of his stipend. But in a case where it is very obvious that the pensioner has suffered an amputation of a limb from a wound received in battle, and has, by reason of his helpless condition, arising from the loss of his limb, delayed his application, it is only just, and entirely consistent with the humane policy of the laws and a liberal construction of the same, that he should receive the pension, at the increased rate, from the time when the amputation took place. Let this be the rule, therefore, in future, in every case where a pensioner has, after being pensioned, suffered the loss of a limb on account of a wound while in the line of his duty as a soldier, receive the benefit of his increased pension from the time when the amputation was made.

W. L. MARCY.

MEXICAN WAR

PENSION OFFICE, *August* 21, 1848.

The following regulations were adopted on the above date, by the Secretary of War, for carrying into effect the provisions of the act of the 21st of July 1848, allowing half pay to widows and orphans of officers and soldiers of the regular army, in certain cases, arising in the war with Mexico.

1. All applicants are required to show, either by the official certificate or testimony of a commissioned officer, or the muster or pay-rolls, or some record evidence from the Adjutant General's Office, that the deceased officer or soldier, on account of whose service the pension is claimed, died of wounds received, or from disease contracted while in the line of his duty, and that he served either in Mexico, or at some post or station on the borders of Mexico. If he did not die in the service, it must be shown that he died while on his return to his usual place of residence in the United States, after having received a discharge upon a surgeon's certificate of disability incurred from wounds received or disease contracted while in the line of duty, or while on his march to join the army in Mexico, or at some post or station on the borders of Mexico.

2. The legality of the marriage, the name of the widow, with those of her children, who may have been under sixteen years of age at the time of the father's decease, with the State or Territory, and county in which she and they reside, should be established. The legality of the marriage may be ascertained by the certificate of the clergyman who joined them in wedlock, or the testimony of respectable persons having knowledge of the fact. The age and number of the children may be ascertained by the deposition of the mother, accompanied by the testimony of respectable persons having knowledge of them, or by transcripts from the parish register, duly authenticated. The widow, at the time of allowing the half pay, or placing her on the list for it, must show that she has not again married; and must, moreover, repeat this at the time of receiving each and every payment thereof; because, in case of her marrying again, the half pay to her ceases, and the half pay for the re-

mainder of the time shall go to the child or children of the deceased widow. This may be done by the affidavits of respectable persons having knowledge of the case.

3. In cases where there are children, and no widow, their guardian will of course act for them, and establish their claims, as prescribed in the foregoing regulations, and receive th eir stipends for them.

4. The credibility of the witness must in every case be certified by the magistrate who may administer the oath; and the official character and signature of the magistrate must be certified by the proper officer, under his seal of office.

5. In every case the applicant, if a widow, must make a declaration according to the form annexed. If there be no widow, and the claim is made on behalf of orphan children, there must be a guardian appointed to act for them, and he must make a declaration, varying the form to suit the case.

J. L. EDWARDS.
Commissioner of Pensions.

☞ The rules of evidence under the law of the 29th of July, 1848, under which widows of Revolutionary soldiers may draw pensions, if married before January 1, 1800, are precisely the same as the rules under the act of 7th of July, 1838, which grants pensions in cases where the marriage took place prior to 1794.

Rules of Evidence relative to half pay due to Virginia Revolutionary officers.

WAR DEPARTMENT, *Pension Office, June* 2, 1835.

Whereas the 4th section of the act of the 3d of March last, entitled "An act to continue the office of the Commissioner of Pensions," directs that the duties heretofore required of and performed by the Secretary of the Treasury in relation to Virginia claims for revolutionary services, and deficiency of commutation be transferred to the Department of War from and after the present month; and the Secretary of War having, by directions from the President of the United States, assigned those duties to the Commissioner of Pensions, notice is hereby given to all concerned, that communications in relation to the claims arising under the act of the 5th July, 1832, entitled "An act to provide for liquidating and paying certain claims of the State of Virginia," will in future be addressed to said Commissioner. The following regulations, which were adopted by the Treasury Department on the 28th July, 1832, to govern the accounting officers of the Treasury, will be adhered to in the settlement of the claims that may be presented at this department under the 3d section of the act of July 5, 1832:

1. The settlement to be confined to those cases of which a list has been furnished by the Auditor of the State of Virginia, as containing the names of those officers reported by the board of officers in 1782 and 1784, (including part of Colonel Crockett's regiment,) whose claims for half pay have not been satisfied, nor prosecuted in court; and of those cases in which judgments have been obtained against, but not paid by the State of Virginia.

2. That sufficient evidence be required as to the identity of the officer on the part of whom or of whose representatives the claim is presented, and that he is still living; or, if dead, of the period of his decease.

3. If the officer is dead, that sufficient proof be required of the existence of heirs and of legal representatives really and lawfully entitled to receive the amount due.

4. Where there are no executors, but administrators, and there are heirs living, that the assent of those heirs be had to the payment of the money to the administrator, or attorney at law, or in fact, who may present himself at the department, or that satisfactory reasons be assigned why such assent be not produced.

5. The administrators in all cases be required to satisfy the accounting officers whether there be or be not heirs living; and, if there be any living, to state their names and residence; and if there be no heirs, to state the the disposition to be made of the amount of the claim.

Executors or Administrators are the legal representatives in claims on account of service in the Virginia State line.

WAR DEPARTMENT, *March* 5, 1836.

SIR: In consequence of the opinion given bp the Attorney General in his communication to this department of yesterday, that the executors or administrators [as the case may be] are the legal representatives contemplated by the act of Congress of the 5th July, 1832, of all deceased officers included in the act, the rule which requires that the assent of the heirs be had to the payment of the money to the administrator or attorney at law, or in fact, is hereby rescinded.

I am, respectfully, LEWIS CASS.

To the COMMISSIONER OF PENSIONS.

Decision of Supreme Court of Appeals of Virginia binding on Department of War, under act of 5th July, 1832.

WAR OFFICE, *August* 16, 1838,

The case of Dr. John Applewhaite, deceased, having been decided by the superior court of Henrico in favor of the claimant, on the principles of the half-pay cases already decided in the supreme court of appeals of the State of Virginia, the decision is, in my opinion, binding upon the department, and there is a legal obligation under the 5th clause of the last section of the act of the 5th July, 1832, to pay the money due the heirs of the deceased Dr. Applewhaite.

J. R. POINSETT.

FORMS.

DECLARATION.

In order to obtain the benefit of the Act of Congress of June 7, 1832, making provision for all who served six months in the Army, Militia, or Navy during the Revolution. (See chap. v., page 12)

STATE, (TERRITORY, OR DISTRICT) OF , } *ss.*
County of

On this day of , personally appeared (*a*) in open court, before the court of , now sitting, A B, a resident (*b*) of in the county of , and State, Territory, or District of aged (*c*) years, who, being first duly sworn according to law, doth, on his oath make the following declaration, in order to obtaiu the benefit of the act of Congress, passed June 7, 1832:

That he entered the service of the United States under the following named officers, and served as herein stated:

[Here set forth the names and rank of the field and company officers; the day (if possible,) and the month and year (*d*) when the claimant entered the service, and the time when he left the same; and if under more than one engagement, he must specify the particular periods, and the rank and names of his officers; the town, the county, or State in which he re sided; when he entered the service; whether he was draughted, was a volunteer, or a substitute; the battles, it any, in which he was engaged; the country through which he marched; the continental regiments or companies with which he served; and the names of some of the regular officers whom he knew; together with such further particulars (*e*) as

(*a*) The declarant must appear in open court, unless prevented from doing so by reason of bodily infirmity; in which case, the declarant will follow the rule laid down for his guidance.

(*b*) The declarant must make his declaration in the county where he resides. If he should fail to do so, he must assign a sufficient reason for not conforming to the rule.

(*c*) The age of the claimant must invariably be mentioned.

(*d*) The declarant must mention the period or periods of the war when he served.

(*e*) Every continental officer or soldier must give the name of the Colonel under whom he served; otherwise, a satisfactory examination of the claim cannot be had. Every claimant must state, with precision, the length of his service, and the different grades in which he served, in language so definite as to enable the department to determine to what amount of pension he is entitled. In a case where the applicant cannot, by reason of the loss of memory, state precisely how long he served, may be useful in the investigation of his claim; and also, if the facts be so, that he has no documentary evidence; and that he knows of no person, whose testimony he can procure, who can testify to his service.]

He hereby relinquishes every claim (*f*) whatever to a pension, or an annuity, except the present, and he declares that his name is not on the pension roll of any agency in any State, or if any only on that of the agency in the State of

Sworn to and subscribed the day and year aforesaid.

A. A.

[And then will follow the certificate the of court.]

And the said court do hereby declare their opinion, (*g*) that the above-named applicant was a revolutionary soldier, and served as he states.

I, , of the court of , do hereby certify (*h*) that the foregoing contains the original proceedings of said court in the matter of the applicatiou of for a pension.

In testimony whereof, I have hereunto set my hand and seal of office (*i*) this day of , &c.

---

he should amend his declaration, by making an affidavit in the following words: "Personally appeared before me, the undersigned, a justice of the peace, &c., A B, who, being duly sworn, deposeth and saith that, by reason of old age, and the consequent loss of memory, he cannot swear positively as to the precise length of his service, but, according to the best of his recollection, he served not less than the periods mentioned below, and in the following grades: For year, months, and days, I served as a . For months and days, I served as a , and for such service I claim a pension."

It is important, in all cases, to determine with precision, the period for which each applicant served, and the particular rank he held, as the law directs the pension to be paid according to the grade of the pensioner and the length of his service. The use of the phrase "*about three or four months*," is too indefinite, and all such qualifying expressions are objectionable. Some persons who apply for pensions merely state that they served two years in the militia, &c., without specifying the tours, the names of the officers, and other particulars respecting their service. This form of a declaration is highly objectionable. It must, in every case, be clearly shown under what officers the applicant served, the duration of each term of engagement, the particular place or places where the service was performed, that the applicant served with an embodied corps called into service by competent authority, that he was either in the field or in garrison, and, for the time during which the service was performed, he was not employed in any civil pursuit."

(*f*) The law makes the relinquishment indispensable.

(*g*) The opinion of the court is always required.

(*h*) The clerk must give his certificate in every case.

(*i*) The clerk must affix his seal; and if it has no device or inscription by which it can be distinguished from any other seal, or if he has no public seal of office, the certificate of a member of Congress, proving the official character and signature of the certifying officer, should accompany the papers.

Mode of authenticating papers.

In every instance where the certificate of the certifying officer who authenticates the papers is not written on the same sheet of paper which contains the affidavit, or other papers authenticated, the certificate must be attached thereto by a piece of tape, or narrow riband, the ends of which must pass under the seal of office of the certifying officer, so as to prevent any paper from being improperly attached to the certificate.

If, on examination of the proper record, the names of applicants making such declaration cannot be found, they will receive detailed instructions respecting the nature and form of the testimony they must produce, to secure their being placed on the pension-roll. *Vide note* (*j*). As the presumption will, in such case, be against the applicants, in consequence of the omission of their names in the muster-rolls, they will be required to furnish, as near as may be, the same evidence as has heretofore been required by the regulations and practice adopted for carrying into effect the act of Congress of March 18, 1818, and the acts supplementary thereto, with such relaxations as have been, from time to time, sanctioned by the department, on account of the rapid decrease of the survivors of the revolutionary army, and the consequent difficulty of procuring direct positive testimony in every case.

Whenever an officer, or non-commissioned officer, is now in the receipt of a pension, he should make application, if entitled to the benefits of this act, by letter merely, setting forth his rank, and the regiment, corps, or vessel, in which he served, and his present place of residence. His pension certificate must accompany his letter.

In those cases where the applicants have once been on the pension-roll, under the act of March 18, 1818, and have been dropped therefrom on account of property, or from any other reason; or where the application has been made under the act of May 15, 1828, and the evidence of service is in the departments; or, having made application and proof of service, and having been rejected, instead of the above declaraton they will make a statement, setting forth, under oath, their having been previously on the pension-roll, and their having been struck from the same, showing their rank, the regiment, corps, or vessel, in which they served, their present place of residence when the first application was made, or of their application under the act of 15th of May, 1828.

In a case where a claimant may make personal application at this department, and can produce satisfactory proof of service, and of his identity also at the seat of government, he may make his declaration before a justice of the peace.

2. The case of the State troops, volunteers, and militia, is different. There are, in the department, no rolls of the State troops, except those of Virginia; and no rolls of the militia, except those of New Hampshire.

Proof of service.

(*j*) In a case where the name of the applicant is not found on the records of the department, he must prove his service by two credible witnesses, who are required to set forth in their affidavits the time of the claimant's entering the service, and the time and manner of his leaving the same, as well as the regiment, company, and line to which he belonged. The magistrate who may administer the oaths must certify to the credibility of the witnesses; and the official character and signature of the magistrate must be certified by the proper officer, under his seal of office.

☞ The notes from (*a*) to (*i*) are all equally applicable to the cases of militiamen, volunteers, and State troops. The proof required by rule, in note (*j*,) applies to continentol troops only, or in militia cases in which muster-rolls exist.

(*k*) This traditionary evidence is indispensable in militia cases.

(*l*) If a witness cannot be found, the declarant must state the fact.

(*m*) The answers to the interrogatories must all be written, and sent to the War Department with the declaration.

Applicants who served in the State troops of Virginia, and applicants who served in the militia of New Hampshire, will be required to produce the same proof as is prescribed for those who served upon the continental establishment. But with respect to the other State troops and militia, there is no record to advert to, and no presumption to be rebutted. The nature of the case, therefore, demands a different rule of proceeding.

Every applicant who claims a pension under the act of June 7, 1832, by virtue of service in the State troops, volunteers, or militia, except as is above provided, will make and subscribe to a declaration in the following form:

STATE, (TERRITORY, OR DISTRICT) OF } ss:
County of }

On this day of , personally appeared (*a*) in open court, before the court of , now sitting, A B, a resident (*b*) of in the county of , and State, Territory, or District of aged (*c*) years, who, being first duly sworn according to law, doth, on his oath make the following declaration, in order to obtain the benefit of the act of Congress, passed June 7, 1832:

That he entered the service of the United States under the following named officers, and served as herein stated:

[Here set forth the names and rank of the field and company officers; the day, (if possible,) and the month and year (*d*) when the claimant entered the service, and the time when he left the same; and if under more than one engagement, he must specify the particular periods, and the rank and names of his officers; the town, the county, or State in which he resided when he entered the service; whether he was draughted, was a volunteer, or a substitute; the battles, if any, in which he was engaged; the country through which he marched; the continental regiments or companies with which he served; and the names of some of the regular officers whom he knew; together with such further particulars (*e*) as may be useful in the investigation of his claim; and also, if the facts be so, that he has no documentary evidence; and that he knows of no person, whose testimony he can procure, who can testify to his service.]

He hereby relinquishes (*f*) every claim whatever to a pension or annuity, except the present; and declares that his name is not on the pension-roll of the agency of any State, or, if any, only on that of the agency of the State of

Sworn to and subscribed the day and year aforesaid.

C. D.

[And then will be annexed the following certificate:)

We, A B, a clergyman, residing in the , and C D, residing in (the same,) hereby certify, that we are well acquainted with

For notes (*a*) (*b*) (*c*) (*d*) (*e*) (*f*) see pages 55 and 56.

, who has subscribed and sworn to the above declaration; that we believe him to be years of age; that he is reputed and believed, in the neighborhood where he resides, to have been a soldier of the revolution; and that we concur in that opinion.

Sworn and subscribed the day and year aforesaid.

[And then will follow the certificate of the court.]

And the said court do hereby declare their opinion (*g*) after the investigation of the matter, and after putting the interrogatories prescribed by the War Department, that the above named applicant was a revolutionary soldier, and served as he states. And the court further certifies, that it appears to them that A B, who has signed the preceding certificate, is a clergyman, resident in the , and that C D, is a credible person; and that their statement is entitled to credit.

I, , clerk (*h*) of the court of , do hereby certify that the foregoing contains the original proceedings of the said court in the matter of the application of for a pension.

In testimony whereof, I have hereunto set my hand and seal (*i*) of office, this day of, &c.

The form of the proceedings, and of the certificates, will be so varied as to meet the case, when the declaration is made out of court, before a judge, as heretofore provided for.

DECLARATION

In order to obtain the benefit of the third section of the act of Congress of the 4th July, 1836, by which widows of Revolutionary officers and soldiers are granted pensions, provided the marriage took place before the expiration of the last period of service. (Chapter IX, p. 15.)

STATE, (TERRITORY, OR DISTRICT) OF , } ss:
County of ,

On this day of , personally appeared before me of the , A B, a resident of , in the county of , and State, (Territory, or District) of , aged years, who, being first duly sworn according to law, doth, on her oath, make the following declaration in order to obtain the benefit of the provision made by the act of Congress passed July 4, 1836: That she is the widow of , who was a [here insert the rank her husband held in the army, navy, or militia, (as the case may be,) and specify the service performed, as directed in rule No. 4 of the regulations.] She further declares that she was married to the said on the

For notes (*g*) (*h*) (*i*) see page 56.

day of , in the year seventeen hundred and ; that her husband, the aforesaid , died on the day of , and that she has remained a widow ever since that period, as will more fully appear by reference to the proof hereto annexed.

Sworn to and subscribed, on the day and year above written, before

---

WAR DEPARTMENT, *Pension Office, March* 15, 1837

In a case where the claimant has married after the decease of the husband, for whose services she may claim the pension, it cannot, under the explanatory act of March 3, 1837, be withheld on account of her last marriage, provided she was a widow on the 4th July, 1836. The latter part of the 6th rule of the regulations of the 9th July, 1836, is not, of course, applicable to such a case. The facts in relation to the marriage of the last husband, and his death, should be fully set forth in the claimant's declaration.

The following is the form of the declaration in such a case:

DECLARATION

In order to obtain the benefits of the third section of the Act of 4th July, 1836, *and of the first section of the Act of* 3d *March,* 1837.

STATE, (TERRITORY, OR DISTRICT) OF } *ss:*
County of }

On this day of , personally appeared before the of the , A B, a resident of , in the county of , and State, [Territory, or District] of , aged years, who being first duly sworn according to law, doth, on her oath, make the following declaration, in order to obtain the benefit of the provision made by the act of Congress passed July 4, 1836, and the act explanatory of said act passed March 3, 1837: That she was married to C D, who was [here insert the particulars respecting the service of the deceased husband for whose services she may claim a pension, as directed in rule No. 4 of the foregoing regulations of July 9, 1836.] She further declares that she was married to the said C D on the day of , in the year seventeen hundred and that her husband, the aforesaid C D, died on the day of ; and that she was afterwards married to H B, who died on the day of ; and that she was a widow on the 4th of July, 1836, and still remains a widow, as will more fully appear by reference to the proof hereto annexed.

Sworn to and subscribed, on the day and year above written, before

---

Form of oath of the Officer who has the record of marriages to be used in claims under the act of July 4, 1836.

In order to prevent any mistake, or improper use that may be made of the affidavit of an officer who may have the custody of records, from which he may make transcripts of the record of a marriage or birth, or the license to celebrate a marriage, the officer who may give his affidavit will, instead of copying the figures contained in the record, write the dates, and at the end of the extract from the records certify "that it is a true copy of the record, with the exception of the date, which is expressed on the record in fair legible figures, as follows:" [Here copy the day, month, and year, in letters and figures, in exact conformity with the original. Then let him add the following words :]

"I, A B, above named, depose and say, that I hold the office of in the county, town, and State aforesaid, and that the above is a true extract from the records of said , with the exception above named, as certified by me.

A B, *Clerk of the*

Sworn before me, C D, *Justice of the Peace.*"

[Then will follow the certificate of the proper officer, under his seal of office, showing that C D is a justice of the peace, commissioner of deeds, notary public, or other officer duly authorized by law to administer oaths.]

☞The oath to be taken before a duly qualified magistrate, whose official character and signature must be certified by the proper officer, under his seal of office. The county clerk, Secretary of State, or some other officer, must certify, under his seal of office, that the officer who administered the oath is a justice of the peace, judge, mayor, alderman, or notary public, (as the case may be,) and that the signature purporting to be his is genuine.

In every case where the clerk of the court or other certifying officer has no public seal of office, the certificate of a member of Congress, proving the official character and signature of the certifying officer, should be sent with the papers.

Mode of authenticating papers.

In every instance where the certificate of the certifying officer who authenticates the papers is not written on the same sheet which contains the affidavit, or other paper authenticated, the certificate must be attached thereto by a piece of tape, or small riband, the ends of which must pass under the seal of office of the certifying officer, so as to prevent any paper from being improperly attached to the certificate.

No affidavit can be admitted as evidence, if not perfectly free from erasure, interlineation, and every other alteration, unless the magistrate who may administer the oath gives a certificate showing that the alteration was made prior to the execution of the paper.

Evidence in cases where Pension Certificates are illegally withheld.

STATE OF
county, } *ss*

Be it known, that before me, a justice of the peace in and for the county aforesaid, personally appeared and made oath, in due form of law, that he is the identical named in an original pension certificate now illegally withheld by

[Here state the facts respecting the detention of the pension certificate.] that he is entitled to a pension of* dollars per month on account of wounds and disabilities received, or of services rendered to the United States during the war; that he served in Captain 's company of , in the regiment; that he now resides in , and has resided there for the space of years past; and that, previous thereto, he resided in

Sworn and subscribed this day of , 18 .

J. P.

NOTE.—The above deposition must be signed by the deponent.

STATE OF } ss.
county, }

Conformably to the regulations of the War Department of the 27th of October, 1832, I, a magistrate in the county above named, do hereby certify that I have the most satisfactory evidence, viz :† that , who this day appeared before me to take the oath of identity, is the identical pensioner he declares himself to be in the annexed affidavit; and I am also satisfied that the statement made by him in relation to the pension certificate is true.

Given under my hand at , the day and year above written.

J. P.

I, , clerk of the court of county, certify that is a magistrate as above, and that the foregoing certificate, purporting to be his, is genuine.

In testimony whereof, I have hereunto affixed my seal of office, and subscribed my name, this day of , in the year

[L. S.] *Clerk of the court of county.*

Application for an increase of pension.

It is hereby certified that formerly a of Captain 's company in the regiment of , who,

*This blank must be filled with the amount to which the pensioner is now entitled, which, in some cases, varies from that in the original certificate.

☞The oath may be administered by any officer properly qualified to take affidavits.

†Here state what the evidence is; whether personal knowledge, or the affidavits of respectable persons—giving their names.

☞The oath may be made before any officer duly authorized to administer oaths.

it appears by the accompanying (*a*) , was placed on the pension-roll at the rate of dollars per month, on account, as he states, of having received a (*b*) while in the line of his duty, and in the said service, on or about the day of , in the year , at a place called , in the State (or Territory) of , is not only still disabled in consequence of the said injury, but, in my opinion is entitled to more than he already receives as a pensioner, being disabled to a degree amounting to (*c*) of a total disability.

} *Surgeons.*

Application for a transfer.

County of , *ss.*

On this day of , 18 , before me, the subscriber, a justice of the peace for the said county of , personally ap-

If the applicant was pensioned on account of a wound received previous to the late war, he should be examined by two surgeons, under a commission issued by a judge of one of the United States.

☞The magistrate who may administer the oaths to the surgeons must certify that they are reputable in their profession; and the official character and signature of the magistrate must be certified by the proper officer under his seal of office.

Mode of authenticating papers.—In every instance where the certificate of the certifying officer who authenticates the papers is not written on the same sheet of paper which contains the affidavit, or other paper authenticated, the certificate must be attached thereto by a piece of tape, or small riband; the ends of which must pass under the seal of office of the certifying officer, so as to prevent any paper from being improperly attached to the certificate.

(*b*) Here give a particular description of the wound, injury, or disease, and specify in what manner it has affected the applicant, so as to produce disability in the degree stated; and show its origin and progress.

(*c*) N. B.—The blank in the last line is to be filled up with the proportional "degree" of disability; for example: "three-fourths," "one-half," "one-third," *&c.*, or "totally," as the case may be.

☞The magistrate who may administer the oaths to the surgeons must certify that they are reputable in their profession; and the official character and signature of the magistrate must be certified by the proper officer, under his seal of office.

If the claimant is within thirty miles of an army surgeon, he must obtain his testimony.

☞No claim to an increase of pension will be examined, unless the proof be first presented to the pension agent where payment is made. He will forward the surgeons' affidavit, pension certificate, &c., to the War Department, with a statement by him that he knows the surgeons to be reputable in their profession, or believes, on the information of others, that they are so.

If the applicant was pensioned on account of a wound received previous to the late war, he should be examined by two surgeons, under a commission issued by a judge of one of the United States courts, in order to obtain an increase of his pension.

peared , who, on his oath, declares that he is the same person who formerly belonged to the company commanded by Captain , in the regiment commanded by Colonel , in the service of the United States; that his name was placed on the pension roll of the State of , from whence he has lately removed; that he now resides in the State (District or Territory) of , where he intends to remain, and wishes his pension to be there payable in future. The following are his reasons for removing from to

Sworn and subscribed to before me, the day and year aforesaid.

☞The oath to be taken before a duly qualified magistrate, whose official charaater and signature must be certified by the proper officer, under his seal of office. The county clerk, Secretary of State, or some other officer, must certify under his seal of office, that the officer who administered the oath is a justice of the peace, judge, mayor, alderman, or notary public, (as the case may be,) and that the signature purporting to be his is genuine.

The oath must be supported by the testimony of some respectable person, as to the pensioner's identity. He must swear that the person who has taken the above oath is the person described in the affidavit. The magistrate must certify that the witness is a person of veracity, and the affidavit must also be authenticated in the manner above directed.

In every case where the clerk of the court, or other certifying officer, has no public seal of office, the certificate of a member of Congress, proving the official character and signature of the certifying officer, should be sent with the papers.

Mode of autheaticrting papers.—In every instance where the certificate of the certifying officer who authenticates the papers is not written on the same sheet which contains the affidavit, or other paper authenticated, the certificate must be attached thereto by a piece of tape, or small riband, the ends of which must pass under the seal of office of the certifying officer, so as to prevent any paper from being improperly attached to the certificate.

Applcation for a new certificate.

County of , *ss.*

On this day of ,18 , before me, the subscriber, a justice of the peace for the said county of , personally appeared , who, on his oath, declares that he is the same person who formerly belonged to the company commanded by Captain , in the regiment commanded by Colonel , in the service of the United States; that his name was placed on the pension roll of the State of , *that he received a certificate of that fact under the signature and seal of the Secretary of War, which certificate, on or about the day of , 18 , at or near he*

Sworn and subscribed to before me, the day and year aforesaid.

NOTES.—The last four blanks are left for the applicant to set forth the time, place, and manner of the loss or destruction of the original certificate.

The oath to be taken before a duly qualified magistrate, whose official character and signature must be properly authenticated.

If the pensioner has never received a formal certificate, but has drawn his pension on a mere notification, (as was the case, in a few instances, many years ago,) he should leave out the above words in *italics*, and insert, in lieu thereof, "*but has never received a formal certificate, and now wishes to obtain one.*"

The pensioner's oath must be supported by another person as to identity. The person must swear that he well knows him to be the same person described in the above affidavit. The magistrate must certify that the deponent is a person of veracity. This oath must also be authenticated by the certificate of the proper officer, under his seal of office, setting forth that the officer before whom the affidavit may be made is a justice of the peace, judge, or notary public, (as the case may be.) When a person acting as an agent or attorney for a pensioner loses the certificate, the affidavit of that person is also required, which must be authenticated as above.

In every case where the clerk of the court or other certifying officer has no public seal of office, the certificate of a member of Congress, proving the official character and signature of the certifying officer, should be sent with the papers.

Mode of authenticating papers.—In every instance where the certificate of the certifying officer who authenticates the papers is not written on the same sheet which contains the affidavit or other paper authenticated, the certificate must be attached thereto by a piece of tape or narrow riband, the ends of which must pass under the seal of office of the certifying officer, so as to prevent any paper from being improperly attached to the certificate.

No attention will be given to applications from persons who act as agents, unless they are known at the War Department, or are vouched for as respectable persons by some one who is known to the department.

DECLARATION.

In order to obtain the benefit of the act of Congress of the 7th July 1838, entitled "An act granting half pay and pensions to certain widows."

STATE, [TERRITORY, OR DISTRICT] OF } *ss.*

On this day of , personally appeared before the of the A B, a resident of , in the county of , aged years, who, being first duly sworn according to law, doth, on her oath, make the following declaration, in order to obtain the benefit of the provision made by the act of Congress, passed July 7, 1838, entitled "An act granting half pay and pensions to certain widows:" that she is the widow of , who was a [here mark the rank the husband held in the army, navy, or militia, as the case may be, and specify the service performed, as directed in rule, numbered one, of these regulations.]

She further declares that she was married to the said on the day of , in the year seventeen hundred and ; that her husband, the aforesaid , died on the day of ; that she was not married to him prior to his leaving the service, but the marriage took place previous to the first of January, seventeen hundred and ninety-four, viz: at the time above stated.

Sworn to and subscribed on the day and year above written, before

---

REGULATIONS OBSERVED IN PAYING NAVY PENSIONS.

The agents for paying navy pensions are directed to observe the following rules:

1st. The identity of the pensioner must be proved by the exhibition of his certificate, and by his oath and signature, before a justice of the peace, or other officer duly qualified to administer oaths, in accordance with the subjoined form, marked A.

2d. If application be made by, or on behalf of a widow, proof of her identity, that she is still living, and has not intermarried, must be furnished according to the form herewith, marked B.

3d. Payments to a guardian will be made on evidence that the child or children are living, and that they are not over sixteen years of age; and a certificate from the proper authority that he is, *at the time*, acting in that capacity, agreeably to the annexed form, marked C.

4th. All pensions unclaimed for two years and upwards, will, previous to payment, be referred by the agent, with all the documents, to the Fourth Auditor of the Treasury for investigation, and, if found correct by the accounting officers, they will be returned to the agent for payment.

5th. No payments of pensions will be made for a less period than six months, either by the agents or the Fourth Auditor, except in the first payments becoming due to pensioners, or where they shall die, or the pension expires, previous to the time for the regular semi-annual payments.

J. L. EDWARDS,
Commissioner of Pensions.

A.

STATE OF } *sct.*
county, }

Be it known, that before me, a * in and for the county aforesaid, personally appeared (*a*) a (*b*) pensioner, and made oath in due form of law that he is the identical named in an original certificate of pension, bearing date at the Navy Department, on the day of , and signed by (*c*) Secretary of the Navy; which certificate he exhibited to me, and by which it appears that he is entitled to a pension of dollars per month.

(*d*)

Sworn and subscribed this day of
before me

Justice of the Peace.

The above deposition must be signed by the deponent, and bear date not more than thirty days anterior to the time of the semi-annual payment.

B

STATE OF } *sct.*
county, }

Be it known, that before me, a *a* in and for the county

Notes to form A.

(*) Justice of the peace, or other officer as the case may be.
(*a*) Name of the pensioner.
(*b*) *Navy or privateer*, as the case may be.
(*c*) Name of the Secretary who issned the certificate.
(*d*) Signature of the deponent.

Notes to form C

(*a*) Justice of the peace, or other officer, as the case may be.

aforesaid, personally appeared (b) widow of (c) and made oath in due form of law, that she is the identical (b) named in an original certificate of pension, bearing date at the Navy Department, on the day of , and signed by (d) Secretary of the Navy; which certificate she exhibited to me, and by which it appears that she is entitled to a pension of dollars per month, and that she has not intermarried, but continues the widow of the above mentioned (c)

(e)

Sworn and subscribed this day of 18 , before me.

Justice of the Peace.

This affidavit must be signed by the deponent, and bear date not more than thirty days anterior to the time of the semi annual payment.

C.

STATE OF
county. } *sct.*

Be it know, that before me, a (a) in and for the county aforesaid, personally appeared (b) guardian of (c) orphan child of (d) and made oath in due form of law, that he is the guardian named in the accompanying certificate of guardianship; that his said wards are the children of (d) referred to in an original certificate of pension, bearing date at the Navy Department, on the day of , and signed by (e) Secretary of the Navy; by which it appears (f) entitled to a pension of dollars per month, and that the said child (g) still living, and not over sixteen years of age.

(h)

Sworn and subscribed this day of 18 , before me.

Justice of the Peace.

(b) Name of the widow.
(c) Name of the deceased husband.
(d) Name of the Secretary who issued the certificate.
(e) Signature of the widow.

Notes to form C.

(a) Justice of the peace, or other officer, as the case may be.
(b) Name of the guardian.
(c) Name of the child or children.
(d) Name of the deceased father.
(e) Name of the Secretary who signed the certificate.
(f) He, she, or they, is or are, as the case may be.
(g) Is or are, as the case may be.
(h) Signature of the guardian.

RULES TO BE OBSERVED IN DRAWING MONEY FROM PENSION AGENTS.

The following instructions and forms, officially issued on January 1, 1847, supersede all former instructions on the same subject. Care has been taken to bring together the detached forms and instructions, which have been prescribed at different times, as occasion required, arranged in their proper order, to conform to existing laws.

From these instructions, applicants or their attorneys, will see the forms in which the claims arising under the various laws, are to be presented.

Pensioners under the War Department.

The following order will be observed in the several documents composing the voucher viz:

1st. When application is made for the payment of a pension, the first thing that seems necessary is, that the identity of the person, in whose behalf the pension is claimed, should be established. This must be done agreeably to the subjoined form, marked A; and for widows pensioned by the War Department, agreeably to form, marked E.

2d. Under the provisions of the acts of 6th April, 1838, and 23d August, 1842, where a pension has remained unclaimed by any pensioner, for the term of *fourteen* months after the same became due and payable, it cannot be paid by the pension agent, but application therefor must be made to the treasury of the United States through the Third Auditor, if the pension certificate issued from the War Department, and through the Fourth Auditor, if it issued from the Navy Department. The usual vouchers will suffice, with the exception that additional proof of the identity of the pensioner will be required, according to form marked B. Each pension agent, immediately on the expiration of fourteen months, subsequent to each semi-annual payment, will certify to the office of the Second Comptroller a correct list, containing the name, rank, rate of pension, amount due, and time of last payment of each pensioner remaining unpaid on the roll of his agency, whose pension has been due and payable for the term of fourteen months prior to the date of such certificate. When, however, a new pensioner is placed on the roll, or an old pension is renewed, the fourteen months commences, running from the semi-annual payment next after the date of his or her pension certificate, and not from the commencement or renewal of the pension.

3d. When an attorney shall make application for a pension, *be the rank of the pensioner what it may*, he must deposite with you a power of attorney in his favor, duly acknowledged, and dated on, or subsequent to the day on which the pension claimed became due, and within ninety days of the time of his applying for payment, and and also his own affidavit that said power was not given him by reason of any *sale*, *transfer*, or *mortgage* of said pension; and the execution of the power must be in the presence of as least one witness, other than the magistrate before whom it is acknowledged. These papers must be made out in strict conformity to the subjoined form, marked C.

4th. In all cases of payments upon a power of attorney, the justice of the peace or magistrate before whom the power is executed, must have lodged with the agent the certificate of the clerk of some court of record, under seal of the court, that he is legally authorized to act as such; and also a paper bearing his proper signature, certified to be such, by the clerk of some court of record.

5th. It is advisable, and is so recommended, that pension agents procure and place in a book the signatures and seals of the clerks of the different courts within their agency, who may be authorized to certify as to powers, the better to detect, by comparison of the signatures and seals, impositions that may be attempted.

6th. Under the provisions of the acts of 2d March, 1829, and 29th June, 1840, in case of the death of any pensioner, the arrears of pension due to him at the time of his death must be paid—

I. "To the widow of the deceased pensioner, or to her attorney," proving herself to be such before a court of record.

II. If there be no widow, then to the executor or administrator on the estate of such pensioner, for the sole and exclusive benefit of the children, to be by him distributed among them in equal shares; and the law of 1840 declares, that the arrears of pension "shall not be considered a part of the assets of said estate, nor liable to be applied to the payment of the debts of said estate in any case whatever."

III. In case of the death of any pensioner who is a widow leaving children, the amount of pension due at the time of her death must be paid to the executor or administrator for the benefit of her children, as directed in the foregoing paragraph.

IV. In case of the death of any pensioner, whether male or female, leaving children, the amount of pension may be paid to any one or each of them, as they may prefer, without the intervention of an administrator. If one of the children is selected to receive the amount due, he, or she, must produce a power of attorney from the others for that purpose, duly authenticated. The oath of identity for the widow, or child, of a deceased pensioner must be according to form, marked F; and when they appoint an attorney, the power of attorney must be according to form marked G.

V. If there be no widow, child, or children, then the amount due such pensioner at the time of his death, must be paid to the legal representatives of the decedent.

VI. When an executor or administrator shall apply for the pension due to a deceased person, he must deposite with you a cetificate of the clerk of the court, judge, of probate, register of wills, ordinary or surrogate, (as the case may be,) stating that he is duly authorized to act in that capacity on the estate of the deceased pensioner, and, if a male, that it has been proved to his satisfaction that there is no widow of the said pensioner living.

7th. In all cases of payments being made of moneys due a deceased pensioner, the original pension certificate must be surrendered, as evidence of the identity of the person to whom the pension claimed was due, or other substantial evidence of such identity must be produced in case such certificate cannot be obtained for surrendry and that due search and inquiryhave been made for for said certificate and that it cannot be found. The date of said pensioner's death must be proved before a court of record.

8th. A certificate of the facts proved must be obtained from the clerk of the court. It is not necessary for the clerk to give the evidence in detail, but only to state the facts that have been proved, and certify under his seal of office, that the testimony adduced was satisfactory to the court, according to form marked H; and in case a pen-certificate is illegally witheld from a pensioner, he (or she as the case may be) must produce evidence of identity and the facts, agreeably to form marked I.

9th. When a pensioner is placed under guardianship, the guardian applying for a pension must, in addition to the evidence of the pensioner's identity, deposit with you a certificate of the proper authority, that he is, *at the time*, acting in that capacity, and also satisfactory evidence that his ward was living at the date the pension claimed became due. The identity of the pensioner in such cases must be established under the form herewith, marked D.

10th. For all payments made by you, duplicate receipts must be taken, (agreeably to subjoined form, marked K,) one of each you will forward with your quarterly accounts, to the Third Auditor of the Treasury for pensions under the War Department, and to the Fourth Auditor for pensions under the Navy Department; and in *all* cases where a pensioner or attorney makes a mark from inability to write his name, there must be a witness thereto, otherwise such receipt, or voucher, will not be admitted at the Treasury.

NOTE.—By the second section of "An act making appropriations for the payment of the revolutionary and other pensioners of the United States," approved February 22d, 1840, pension agents are authorized to administer all oaths required to be administered to pensioners, attorneys of pensioners, or others, in the course of the preparation of papers for the payment of pensions under any of the laws of Congress; and to charge and receive the same compensation therefor as the laws of the State in which the agent is located allow to magistrates for similar services.

A.

STATE OF } *ss.*
county, }

Be it known, that before me, a in and for the county aforesaid, duly authorized by law to administer oaths, personally appeared and made oath in due form of law, that he is the identical person named

Note.—The above deposition must be signed by the deponent.

Where the pension has been increased, since the certificate has been given, the magistrate will note that fact.

In the case of a *revolutionary* pensioner, the part of the above form which requires the pensioner to depose that "he has not been employed, or paid, &c.," is not required. The law of April 30, 1844, forbids the payment of an invalid pension to any person while in either of the military services, "unless the disability, for which the pension was granted, be such as to have occasioned his employment in a lower grade."

in an original certificate in his possession, of which (I certify) the following is a true copy:

(*Here insert a copy of his certificate of pension.*)

that he now resides in , and has resided there for the space of years past; and that previous thereto he resided in ; and that he has not been employed, or paid, in the army, navy, or marine service of the United States from the day of to

Sworn and subscribed this
day of 18
before me.

B.

STATE OF ,
county of ,
18

I , a magistrate in the county above named, do hereby certify that I have the most satisfactory evidence,* viz: that , who has this day appeared before me to take the oath of identity, is the identical person named in the pension certificate, which he has exhibited before me, numbered , and bearing date at the War Office, the day of , 18 ; and signed by , *Secretary of War.*

Given under my hand, at on the day and year above written.

J. P.

STATE OF , ss.
county,

I , clerk of the court, of the county and State aforesaid, do hereby certify that is a justice of the peace, in and for said county, duly commissioned and qualified; that his commission was dated on the day of , 18 , and will expire on the day of , 18 , and that his signature above written is genuine.

[L. S.] Given under my hand and the seal of said county, this day of , 18 .

Clerk.

*Here state what the evidence is; whether personal knowledge, or the affidavits of respectable persons, giving their names.

Note.—Where the pensioner is personally known to the agent, and he will certify to his identity, the above form (B.) may be dispensed with.

C.

Know all men by these presents, that I ‘ of (*a*) pensioner of the United States, do hereby constitute and appoint my true and lawful attorney, for me, and in my name, to receive from the agent of the United States for paying pensions in , State of , my pension from the day of 18 , to the day of 18 . Witness my hand and seal, this day of , 18 .

Sealed and delivered }
in presence of }

[L. S.]

STATE OF , } ss.
county, }

Be it known, that on the of , 18 , before the subscriber, a in and for said county, duly authorized by law to administer oaths, personally appeared , above named, and acknowledged the foregoing power of attorney to be his act and deed. In testimony whereof, I have hereunto set my hand the day and year last above mentioned.

STATE OF , } ss.
county, }

Be it known, that on the day of , 18 , before me, a in and for said county, duly authorized by law to administer oaths, personally appeared , the attorney named in the foregoing power of attorney, and made oath that he has no interest whatever in the money he is authorized to receive, by virtue of the foregoing power of attorney, either by any pledge, mortgage, sale, assignment, or transfer, and that he does not know or believe that the same has been so disposed of to any person whatever.

Sworn and subscribed, the day and year last above mentioned.
Before me.

D.

STATE OF , } ss.
county, }

Be it known, that before me, , a in and for said county, duly authorized by law to administer oaths, per-

Note.—The above form of oath is *necessary* for the attorneys of widows pensioned under the laws of July 4, 1836, and July 7, 1838, and subsequent laws continuing their provisions. For other pensions, the old form of attorney's oath is sufficient; but as the above is valid in *all* cases, to prevent mistakes, its general adoption is advised.

Note.—This affidavit must be signed by the attorney.

(*a*) In this blank insert the word invalid, or revolutionary, as the case may be.

Note.—Any other officer duly authorized to administer oaths, may be substituted for a justice of the peace.

sonally appeared , guardian of , and made oath in due form of law that the said is still living, and is the identical person named in the original certificate in his possession, of which (I certify) the following is a true copy;

(Here insert a copy of his certificate of pension.)

That he now resides in , and has resided there for the space of years past, and that previous thereto he resided in

Guardian.

Sworn and subscribed this day of , 18 , before me.

E.

Form of an affidavit to be made by a widow placed on the pension-rolls of the War Department.

STATE, [OR TERRITORY] OF , } *ss.*
County of , }

Be it known, that before me, , a , duly, authorized by law to administer oaths, in and for the county aforesaid personally appeared , and made oath in due form of law, that she is the identical person named in an original certificate in her possession, of which (I certify) the following is a trne copy:

(Here insert a copy of her certificate of pension.)

that she has not intermarried, but continues the widow of the above mentioned ; and that she now resides in , and has resided there for the space of years past; and that previous thereto she resided in , of the truth of which statements I am fully satisfied.

Sworn to and subscribed this day of , I83 , before me.

Note.—The above deposition must be signed by the deponent.

[In cases where a widow was placed on the pension-roll under the act of March 3d, 1843, and *had surrendered her certificate* on the expiration of her pension previously to the renewal of widows' pensions by the act of June 17, 1844, the following form may be substituted for the above. But as widows who were never placed on the pension list prior to the act of June 1844, whose claims have subsequently been admitted, will be furnished with pension certificates from the War Department *they* will be required to set out a copy of their certificates in the oath of identity, agreeably to the foregoing form.]

$

United States of America

STATE OF , } ss.
county,

Be it known, that before me, a in and for the county aforesaid, duly authorized by law to administer oaths, personally appeared , and made oath in due form of law, that she is the identical person who drew a pension under the act of the 3d of March, 1843, on account of the revolutionary service of her husband, the late [here give the name and rank of the husband] at the rate of $ per annum; that she now makes this affidavit for the purpose of drawing a pension under the act of Congress passed on the 17th of June, 1844, entitled "An act to continue the pensions of certain widows;" that she has not intermarried, but continues to be a widow; that she now resides in , in the county of , and State of , and has resided there for the space of years past; and that previous thereto she resided in

Sworn to and subscribed this day of 184

In presence of

Before me

I certify that the above-named affiant is personally known to me, and that she is the same individual who drew a pension as stated by her in the foregoing affidavit.

Justice of the Peace, or other magistrate.

F

Oath of identity for the widow or child of a deceased pensioner.

STATE OF , }
county,

Be it known, that before me , a in and for the county aforesaid, duly authorized by law to administer oaths, personally appeared , and made oath in due form of law, that she, (or he, as the case may be) is the widow (or son, or daughter, as the case may be) of the identical person who was a pensioner, and is now dead, and to whom a certificate of pension was issued, which is herewith surrendered

That the deceased pensioner resided in , in the State of for the space of years before his death; and that previous thereto he resided in .

Sworn and subscribed this day of , 18 , before me

Note.—The above deposition must be signed by the deponent. Where the pension has been increased, since the certificate has been given, the magistrate will note the fact.

Note.—The oath of identity for the executor or administrator of a deceased pensioner may be in the foregoing form substituting "executor" (or "administrator" as the case may be) for "widow" &c.

G

Power of attorney for the widow or child of a deceased pensioner.

Know all men by these presents, that I, , of , in the county of , State of widow, (or child, as the case may be,) of , who was (*a*) pensioner of the United States, do hereby constitute and appoint my true and lawful attorney, for me, and in my name, to receive from the agent of the United States for paying pensions in , State of , the balance of said pension from the day of 18 , to the day of , 18 , being the day of his death.

Witness my hand and seal, this day of , 18 .

Sealed and delivered in presence of [L. S.]

Note.—The forms of acklowledgment of the above power, and of the attorney's oath are the same as in form C. When one of the children is appointed by the others to receive the balance, the attorney's oath is not required.

(*a*) In this blank insert the word invalid, or revolutionary, as the case may be.

H.

Certificate of the Court as to the death of a pensioner.

STATE OF , } *ss.*
county of ,

I, , clerk of the court of , holden at , in and for , do hereby certify that satisfactory evidence has been exhibited to said court that was a pensioner of the United States at the rate of dollars per ; was a resident of the county of , in the State of , and died in the , in the State of , in the year , on the day of ; that he left a widow [or no widow] (or child or children, as the case may be) whose name is (or are, as the case may be.)*

In testimony whereof, I have hereunto set my hand and affixed my seal of office, at , this [Seal of the court.] day of , in the year of our Lord 18 .

Clerk of the .

*In case the pension certificate has been lost, insert, immediately after the name, or names, of the widow, child or children, as the case may be, the following; "And that the pension certificate of said pensioner has been lost, and, after due search and inquiry therefor, it cannot be found."

I.

Evidence in cases where Pension Certificates are illegally withheld.

STATE OF , *county,* } ss.

Be it known, that before me, , a in and for the county aforesaid, duly authorized by law to administer oaths, personally appeared . and made oath in due form of law, that he (or she, as the case may be) is the identical named in an original pension certificate now illegally withheld by

[*Here state the facts respecting the detention of the pension certificate,*]

that he (or she) is entitled to a pension of* dollars per month; that he (or she) now resides in , and has resided there for the space of years past; and that, previous thereto, he (or she) resided in

Sworn and subscribed this day of , 18

Note.—The above deposition must be signed by the deponent.

—

STATE OF , *county,* } ss.

Conformably to the regulations of the War Department of the 27th of October, 1832, I, , a magistrate in the county above named, do hereby certify that I have the most satisfactory evidence, viz:† that , who, this day appeared before me to take the oath of identity, is the identical pensioner he (or she) declares himself (or herself) to be in the annexed affidavit; and I am also satisfied that the statement made by him (or her) in relation to the pension certificate is true.

Given under my hand at , the day and year above written.

I, , clerk of the court of county, certify that is a magistrate as above, and that the foregoing certificate, purporting to be his, is genuine.

In testimony whereof, I have hereunto affixed my seal of office, and [L. S.] subscribed my name, this day of , in the year .

Clerk of the court of county.

*This blank must be filled with the amouut to which the pensioner is now entitled, which, in some cases, varies from that in the original certificate.

☞The oath may be administered by any officer properly qualified to take affidavits.

†Here state what the evidence is; whether personal kuowledge, or the affidavits of respectable persons—giving their names.

☞The oath may be made before any officer duly authorized to administer oaths. If the pension agent act as magistrate in the case, the certificate of the clerk of the court is not reqnired.

K.

18 .

Received of , agent for paying pensions, dollars cents, being for month's pension due to from the day of , 18 , to the day of 18 , for which I have signed duplicate receipts.

$

PENSION OFFICE, *March* 9, 1848.

In order to carry into effect the act of Congress renewing the pensions of widows under the act of February 2, 1848, the applicant who may claim a pension, must make a declaration, under oath, before some magistrate in the county where she resides, which declaration must be duly authenticated. The official character and signature of the magistrate must be certified by the pro per officer under his seal of office, and the magistrate must certify that the declarant is peisonally known to him.

J. L. EDWARDS,
Commissiomer of Pensions.

Declaration in order to obtain the benefits of the Act of Congress of 2d February, 1848, *entitled "An act making further provision for surviving widows and soldiers of the Revolution.*

STATE, [TERRITORY, OR DISTRICT,] OF } *ss.*

On this day of personally appeared before the , of the , A. B., a resident of , in the county of , aged years, who being first duly sworn, according to law, doth on her oath, make the following declaration, in order to obtain

NOTE.—It will be perceived that the act of the 2d February, 1848, provides as well for widows of officers and soldiers of the Revolution who may hereafter die, as for those who have already died. Many widows, therefore, will be entitled to the provisions of the act of 1848, who have not drawn, or been entitled to, any pension under any former law. They will vary their declarations to conform to the circumstances of their cases. If their husband's have been pensioned, they will state the fact, with such particulars in relation to his residence, and amount of pension, as the foregoing form directs.

If neither the applicant nor her husband has been pensioned, she will be required to make such proofs as the regulations require under the act of the 7th July, 1838, the benefits of the provision made by the act of Congress, passed on the 2d February, 1848, granting pensions to widows of persons who served during the revolutionary war. That she is the widow of , who was a (here insert the rank the husband held in the army, navy, or militia, as the case may be, and the regiment, corps, or vessel, in which he served, and the annual amount of the pension which she received under the act of 17th June, 1844.)

She further declares that she is still a widow.

Sworn to and subscribed on the day and year above written, before

---

Declaration in order to obtain the benefit of the Act of the 21st July, 1848.

STATE, [TERRITORY, OR DISTRICT] of } ss.

On this day of , personally appeared before the of the A B, a resident of in the county , and State, [Territory, or District] of aged years, who being first duly sworn according to law, doth on her oath make the following declaration, in order to obtain the benefit of the provision made by the law of the United States, passed on the 21st of July, 1848: That she is the widow of , who was a in the regiment of United States ; that she was married to the said on the day of , in the year eighteen hundred and ; that her husband, the aforesaid , died on the day of at , in , in consequence of , and that she has remained a widow ever since that period, as will more fully appear by reference to the proofs hereto annexed.

Sworn to and subscribed on the day and year above written, before

[Magistrate's signature.] [Declarant's signature.]

☞The official character and signature of the magistrate must be certified by the proper officer, under his seal of office.

Widow's Declaration in order to obtain the benefit of the Act of Congress of the 29th July, 1848.

STATE, [TERRITORY OR DISTRICT] OF }

On this day of , personally appeared before the of the , A B, a resident of , in the county of , aged years, who, being duly sworn, according to law, doth, on her oath, make the following declaration, in order to obtain the benefit of the provisions made by the act of Congress, passed , who was a [here insert the rank the husband held in the army, navy, or militia, as the case may be, and specify the service performed, as directed in rule numbered one of these regulations.]

She further declares that she was married to the said on the day of , in the year seventeen hundred and ; that her husband, the aforesaid died on the day of ; that she was not married to him prior to his leaving the service, but the marriage took place previous to the second of January, eighteen hundred, viz: at the time above stated, She further swears that she is now a widow, and that she has never before made any application for a pension.

Sworn to and subscribed on the day and year above written, before

---

Application of a Widow in order to renew her pension.

To the COMMISSIONER OF PENSIONS:

The memorial of the undersigned, the widow of the late who was a in the Navy of the United States, respectfully shows:

That her husband, the aferesaid entered the service of the United States, in the year ; that while in the said service, and holding the rank above mentioned, he departed this life, at , on the day of , in the year ; that the undersigned was married to the said on the day of , in the year ; and in proof thereof, she refers to papers on file in the Pension Office, upon which she obtained a pension for five years. She therefore claims the benefits of the act of Congress of the 11th of August, 1848, granting pensions to the widows of officers, seamen, and marines, who have died in the service aforesaid; and she requests that her name may be inscribed on the roll of pensioners under that law who are paid at , in the State of

Sworn and subscribed to before me, on this day of , in the year

---

Surgeons' Certificate in an invalid case.

(Date.)

It is hereby certified that , a in the United States ship of war , commanded by , is rendered incapable of performing the duty of a , by reason of wounds or other injuries inflicted while he was actually in the service aforesaid, and in the line of his duty, viz:

By satisfactory evidence, and accurate examination, it appears that on the day of , in the year , being engaged and he is thereby [not only incapacitated for duty aforesaid, but, in the opinion of the undersigned is disabled from obtaining his subsistence from manual labor.

Surgeon.

Assistant Surgeon.

Certficate of the commanding Officer in an invalid case.

UNITED STATES SHIP ,

184 .

I hereby certify that , who was a on board of this ship, while under my command, and while enaged in his duty as a , was, in consequence of the following circumstances, so injured as to be prevented from any further performance of his duty as a , and I therefore deemed it proper that he should be discharged from the naval service of the United States. He was accordingly discharged on the day of , in the year 184 .

While he was

Regulations under Act of March 3, 1845.

To the COMMISSIONER OF PENSIONS:

The memorial of the undersigned, the widow of the late who was a in the Navy of the United States, respectfully shows :

That her husband, the aforesaid , entered the service of the United States in the year ; that, while in said service, and holding the rank above mentioned, he departed this life, at* , on the day of in the year ; that the undersigned was married to the said on the day of in the year ; and in proof thereof, she refers to papers on file in the Pension Office, upon which she obtained a pension for five years. She therefore claims the benefits of the act of Congress of the 3d of March, 1845, granting pensions to the widows of officers, seamen and marines, who have died in the service aforesaid; and she requests that her name may be inscribed on the roll of pensioners under that law, who are paid at , in the State of

Sworn and subscribed to, before me, on this day of, in the year

---

Application of a Widow who applies for a Pension for the first time.

To the COMMISSIONER OF PENSIONS:

The memorial of the undersigned, the widow of the late who was a , in the Navy of the United States, respectfully shows:

That her husband, the aforesaid , entered the service of the United States in the year ; that,

*If at a navy yard, the fact must be stated, and the name of the navy yard, if on board of a vessel of war, the name of the vessel must be given.

☞The official character and signature of the magistrate who may administer the oath, must be certified by the proper officer, under his seal of office.

while in the said service, and holding the rank above mentioned, he departed this life, at* on the day of , in the year ; that the undersigned was married to the said on the day of , in the year ; and in proof thereof she exhibits the following evidence: [Here describe the proof, whether the clergyman's certificate, the family record, town or county clerk's certificate, or the affidavit of a respectable witness.] She therefore claims the benefits of the acts of Congress, of the 11th August, 1848, granting pensions to the widows of officers, seamen and marines, who have died in the service aforesaid; and she requests that her name may be inscribed on the roll of pensioners under that law who are paid at in the State of

Sworn and subscribed to, before me
on this day of
in the year

*If at a navy yard, the fact must be stated, and the name of the navy yard; if on board of a vessel of war, the name of the vessel must be given.

☞The official character and signature of the magistrate who may administer the oath must be certified by the proper officer, under his seal of office.

☞In no case can the claim be allowed, unless it can be clearly shown by the certificate of a navy surgeon that the husband died of a disease contracted, or of some casualty, by drowning, or otherwise, or of an injury received, while he was in the line of his duty. The surgeon must make a particular statement of all the facts in the case, describe the disorder or injury, and state also upon what particular duty the husband was engaged when the disability arose which resulted in his death.

BOUNTY LANDS.

CHAPTER I.

Land granted to Recruits.

The 4th section of the act of January 20, 1813 provided, that there should be given to each effective, able bodied man, who should enlist into the service of the United States, after the first day of February, 1813, to serve for five years, or during the war, in addition to his pay, the bounty of 160 acres of land previously authorized by law.

CHAPTER II.

The amount of Land doubled.

By the act of December 10, 1814, sec. 4, it was enacted, that in lieu of the 160 acres then allowed by law, there shall be allowed to each non-commissioned officer and soldier, thereafter enlisted, when discharged from service, and who shall have obtained from the commanding officer of his company, battalion, or regiment, a certificate that he had faithfully performed his duty whilst in service, *three hundred and twenty acres of land.* It also provided, that the widow or children, or if no widow or child, the *parents* of every non-commissioned officer or soldier, enlisted according to law, and who were killed or died in the service of the United States, shall be entitled to the said 320 acres of land. It cannot, however, pass to collateral relations.

CHAPTER III.

Time of application for Bounty Lands for service in the War of 1812 with Great Britain, extended.

By the act of June 26, 1848, the time of application for bounty land for service in the war of 1812 with Great Britain, was extended for five years from the date of the passage of the act.

NOTE.—Soldiers to be entitled to bounty for the above named service, must have enlisted for *five years* or during the war.

CHAPTER IV.

New Lands may be selected.

By the act of July 25, 1848, it was enacted, that soldiers of the war of 1812, may within five years from the passage of said act, select new land, if the first warrant was located on land "unfit for location": *Provided*, that before receiving such new land, it shall be proved to the satisfaction of the Commissioner of the General Land Office, that the land is unfit for cultivation, and that said soldier has never disposed of his interest in it by any sale of his own, and that it has not been taken or disposed of for his debts, etc.

MEXICAN WAR BOUNTY LANDS.

CHAPTER V.

The 9th section of the act of February 11, 1847, enacted, that each non-commissioned officer, musician, or private, enlisted or to be enlisted in the regular army, or regularly mustered in any volunteer company, for a period of not less than twelve months, who has served or may serve during the present war with Mexico, and who shall receive an honorable discharge, or who shall have been killed or died of wounds received or sickness incurred in the course of such service, or who shall have been discharged before the expiration of his term of service in consequence of wounds received or sickness incurred in the course of such service, shall be entitled to receive a certificate of warrant from the War Department for the quantity of one hundred and sixty acres, and which may be located by the warrantee, or his heirs at law, at any land office of the United States, in one body, and in conformity to the legal subdivisions of the public lands, upon any of the public lands in such district then subject to private entry; and upon the return of such certificate or warrant, with evidence of the location thereof having been legally made, to the General Land Office, a patent shall be issued therefor. That in the event of the death of any such non-commissioned officer, musician, or private, during service, or after his discharge, and before the issuing of a certificate or warrant as aforesaid, the said certificate or warrant shall be issued in favor and inure to the benefit of his family or relatives, according to the following rules: first, to the widow and to his children; second, his father; third, his mother. And in the event of his children being minors, then the legally constituted guardian of such minor children shall, in conjunction with such of the children, if any, as may be of full age, upon being duly authorized by the orphans, or other court having probate jurisdiction, have power to sell, and dispose of such certificate or warrant for the benefit of those interested. And all sales, mortgages, powers, or other instruments of writing, going to affect the title or claim to any such bounty right, made or executed prior to the issue of such warrant or certificate, shall be null and void to all intents and purposes whatsoever; nor shall such claim to bounty right be in anywise affected by, or charged with, or subject to, the payment of any debt or claim incurred by the soldier prior to the issuing of such certificate or warrant: *Provided,* that no land warrant issued under the provisions of this act shall be laid upon any lands of the United States to which there shall be a pre-emption right, or upon which there shall be an actual settlement and cultivation: *Provided, further,* That every such non-commissioned officer, musician, and private who may be entitled under the provisions of this act to receive a certificate or warrant for one hundred and sixty acres of land, shall be allowed the option to receive such certificate or warrant, or a treasury scrip for one hundred dollars; and such scrip, whenever it is preferred, shall be issued by the Secretary of the Treasury to such person or persons as would be authorized to receive such certificates or warrants for lands; said scrip to bear an interest of six per cent. per annum, payable semi-annually, redeemable at the pleasure of the government. And that each private, non-commissioned officer, and musician, who shall have been received into the service of the United States since the commencement of the war with Mexico, for less than twelve months, and shall have served for such term, or until honorably discharged, shall be entitled to receive a warrant for forty acres of land, which may be subject to private entry, or twenty-five dollars in scrip if preferred; and in the event of the death of such volunteer during his term of service, or after an honorable discharge, but before the passage of this act, then the warrant for such land, or scrip, shall issue to the wife, child, or children, if there be any, and if none, then to the father, and if there be no father, then to the mother of such deceased volunteer: *Provided,* that nothing contained in this section shall be so construed as to give bounty lands to such volunteers as were accepted into sevice, and discharged without being marched to the seat of war.

CHAPTER VI.

Surgeon's Certificate sufficient evidence that the disability arose in the service.

By the joint resolution of March 24, 1848, it was provided, that in all cases of application for bounty land warrants under the act of February 11, 1847, the honorable discharge of the applicant, shewing the same was predicated on a surgeon's certificate of disability, shall be considered as satisfactory evidence to the Commissioner of Pensions, that the disability was incurred in the course of service.

CHAPTER VII.

No Fees required for location.

The act of May 17, 1848, declared, that fees to Registers or Receivers shall not be required from soldiers, who locate their land warrants; although fees are allowed when the location is made by other holders.

CHAPTER VIII.

Brothers and Sisters of Soldiers of the Mexican War, entitled to land in certain cases.

The act of May 27, 1848, provided, that the term "relative" in the 9th section of the act of February 11, 1847, should be considered as extending to the brothers and sisters of those whose services under the act (in the Mexican War,) entitled them to the land therein provided: the order or priority of right, however, to remain as declared by the said act of February 11, 1847. It was also provided, that the benefits of the act of February 11, 1847, should not be construed as forfeited by the privates and non-commissioned officers, who were promoted to the grade of commissioned officers during the Mexican War, and who subsequently fulfilled the condition of their engagement, provided that such promotion was made subsequent to the original organization of the company, corps, or regiment.

CHAPTER IX.

Enlisted men of the Ordnance Corps entitled to land and pensions in certain cases.

The act of July 10, 1848, provided, that the enlisted men of the ordnance department, who served in the Mexican War, should receive the same bounty land as is given to the other regular troops in the service. It also placed them, with regard to disabilities or wounds, on the same footing as the regular army.

NOTE.—The joint resolution of the 10th of August, 1848, places all the officers, non-commissioned officers, musicians, and privates of the Marine Corps who served with the army in the war with Mexico, as also the artificers and laborers of the Ordnance Corps serving in said war, on a footing in all respects as to bounty land and other remuneration, in addition to ordinary pay, with the officers, non-commissioned officers, musicians, and privates of the army, provided that this remuneration shall be in lieu of prize money and all other extra allowances.

CHAPTER X.

Miami Lands in Indiana.

The act of August 7, 1848, allows pre-emption claimants upon the Miami lands in Indiana, entitled to bounty lands, to apply their warrants for services in the Mexican war in payment thereof.

CHAPTER XI.

Location of Bounty Land Warrants' legal subdivision authorized in certain cases.

The act of August 14, 1848, provides, that any non-commissioned officer or soldier, or his widow, may locate his land warrant on any public land subject to private entry, taking the land at the price at which it is subject to private entry, and reckoning the warrant at one dollar and twenty-five cents per acre for the number of acres therein contained, and paying the balance, if any, in money; but no claim to exist on the Government to pay for any balance on said warrant in money.

FORMS AND REGULATIONS FOR OBTAINING MEXICAN BOUNTY LAND WARRANTS.

PENSION OFFICE, *March* 4, 1847.

In order to carry into effect the provisions of the ninth section of the act of the 11th ot February, 1847, the Secretary of War has directed that the following regulations sh allbe observed.

It will be observed, on reading the ninth section of the law, that there are six classes of persons provided for, viz:

1. Those non-commissioned officers, musicians, and privates of the regular army who have served in Mexico during the war with that country, and who have served out the full period of their enlistment, and have been honorably discharged, or who may have been or may be honorably discharged before the expiration of the period of their enlistment, in consequence of wounds received, or sickness incurred, in the course of such service.

2. The representatives of such persons as are men-

tioned in the preceding paragraph, who may die in the service, or after being discharged, and before the issuing of a certificate or warrant.

3. Non-commissioned officers, musicians, and privates, who have been mustered, or may be mustered for twelve months, in any volunteer company, who have served, or may serve, until the end of the war with Mexico, and have been, or may be, honorably discharged by reason of the expiration of their enlistment, or in consequence of disability from wounds received, or sickness incurred, in said service.

4. The representatives, as designated by this act, of such volunteers as shall have died, or may die, in the service, or after having been honorably discharged, and before the issuing of a warrant or certificate.

5. Volunteers received into the service since the commencement of the Mexican war, for less than twelve months, who shall have marched to the seat of war, and shall have served until honorably discharged.

6. The representatives, as designated in the act, of volunteers received into the service for less than three months, and who may have died in the service, or after having been honorably discharged, and defore the passage of this act.

In order to substantiate a claim for land or scrip, under the provisions of the foregoing section of the act, the persons described in the first class of these regulations will send to, or deposite with the Commissioner of Pensions, Washington city, evidence of enlistment, service, and honorable discharge, as required by law. The best evidence on these points is held to be the original discharge of the applicant, which must, in all cases, be produced if in existence, accompanied by the applicant's affidavit (vide form marked A,) setting forth that he is the identical person mentioned in the discharge; and in case of the loss or destruction of the discharge, the applicant will make oath to the fact, and produce the affidavit of some creditable witness in corroboration of his statement. The claimant must set forth the regiment and company to which he belonged; the time of entering the service, the time, place, and manner of his leaving the same, and he must show by the testimony of a commissioned officer that he was honorably discharged.

In case the claimant should desire scrip instead of land, he must make his request in writing according to the form marked B, accompanying these regulations.

The rules in the paragraphs immediately preceding are applicable to volunteers mentioned in classes Nos. 3 and 5.

The representatives of deceased soldiers and others, as mentioned in classes 2, 4, and 6, must produce evidence of the enlistment, service and death of the original claimant. If the soldier was discharged, the discharge must be produced, if in existence. If not, the same proof will be required as in other cases of lost discharges; and if he died in the service, the certificate of his captain or other officer who commanded the company to which he belonged, must be produced.

The persons who may claim must produce evidence of their relationship to the deceased, and show the degree of consanguinity they bore to him. This proof must be drawn in conformity with the form marked C, and may be taken before any court having probate jurisdiction. In case the father claims, he must show that no wife or child of the deceased is living; and in case the mother claims, she must show that neither the wife, child, nor father of the deceased is living.

J. L. EDWARDS,
Commissioner of Pensions.

A.

STATE OF ,
County of ,

On this day of , in the year one thousand eight hundred and , personally appeared before me, the undersigned, a justice of the peace for the county and above mentioned, who being duly sworn according to law, declares that he is the identical who was a in the company commanded by Captain , in the regiment , commanded by that he enlisted on the day of for the term of , and was discharged at on the day of , by reason of

Sworn to and subscribed before me the day and year above written.

☞See notes following:

☞The discharge of a soldier, if he has one, must in every case accompany the above affidavit.

NOTES.

1. It is proper to state, for the information of claimants under the 9th section of the act of February 11, 1847, that, in every instance in which a volunteer soldier was discharged on a surgeon's certificate, that paper must be sent to the Pension Office, with the claimant's affidavit, unless it has been otherwise disposed of. If lost, he should state the fact under oath.

2. The official character and signature of the magistrate who may administer an oath, must be certified by the proper officer, under his seal of office. The certificate must accompany every case, and be attached to the paper on which the affidavit is written. No affidavit taken before a notary public can be admitted as evidence; except in the States of New Hampshire, Connecticut, Virginia, South Carolina, Wisconsin, and Indiana, in which States laws have passed giving such officers power to administer oaths for general purposes.

3. The relinquishment of the right to bounty land must be signed by the claimant, if he wishes to receive scrip in lieu of land, and the relinquishment must be witnessed by some one who writes a legible hand.

4. Volunteers in some cases have been discharged from the service without ever having received a certificate to that effect from the officer who discharged them. Such cases have occurred where an entire regiment has been mustered out of the service. In such a case the claimant must make the oath of identity required by the regulations, and add to the statement as to his service, the following words: "I never received any discharge. The regiment to which I belonged was mustered out of the service."

5. No assignment of land or scrip can be made until after a land warrant has been issued from the Pension Office, or a certificate of scrip, as the case may be.

6. As there were some six months' volunteers, who did not march to the seat of war, it is indispensably necessary that every soldier who was so engaged, should produce the certificate of the commanding officer of the regiment or company to which he belonged, showing that he was at the seat of war. The post to which the soldier marched should be mentioned.

B.

(Date)

Sir: I request that my claim to bounty land, under the ninth section of the act of the 11th of February, 1847, entitled "An act to raise for a limited time an additional military force, and for other purposes," may be examined; and if I am entitled to land, I wish to relinquish, and do hereby relinquish my right thereto, and in lieu thereof to receive a treasury scrip for one hundred dollars.*

I am, respectfully, your obedient servant,

To the Commissioner of Pensions,
Washington City.

C.

It is hereby certified that satisfactory proof has been exhibited before the† for the county of in the State of by the affidavits of and who are persons entitled to credit, that and are the only surviving‡ children of who was a in the United States service.

In testimony whereof I have set my hand and seal of office this day of in the year

*Or twenty-five dollars, as the case may be.

†The evidence may be taken before any officer authorized by law to administer an oath for general purposes.

‡If there be no children, and the father claims, the facts must be stated, and the form will be varied to suit the case; and if there be neither child nor father living, and the widow claims, the form will be so changed as to show the facts in the case.

☞Under the act of May 27, 1848, brothers and sisters may claim, provided the soldier left neither father, mother, widow, nor child. The foregoing form will be varied to suit the case. If a father claims, he must prove by two credible and disinterested witnesses that he is the father, and that the soldier, his son, left neither widow nor child. If a mother claims, she must show that the soldier left neither father, widow, nor child. If a brother claims, he must prove that the soldier left neither father, mother, widow, child, nor sister, and that he is the only surviving brother. The evidence will be varied to suit the case, if more than one brother applies, or sisters and brothers, or a sister or sisters only. In every case it must be clearly shown that the persons who apply are the only heirs under the acts of February 11, 1847, and May 27, 1848.

*If at a navy yard, the fact must be stated, and the name of the navy yard; if on board of a vessel of war, the name of the vessel must be given.

☞The official character and signature of the magistrate who may administer the oath, must be certified by the proper officer, under his seal of office.

BOUNTY LAND

FOR THE SOLDIERS OF THE WAR WITH GREAT BRITAIN IN 1812, OR IN ANY OF THE INDIAN WARS SINCE 1790.

CHAPTER XII.

On the 28th of September, 1850, *the following Act was passed:*

Be it enacted, That each of the surviving, or the widow or minor children of deceased commissiond and non-commissioned officers, musicians, or privates, whether of regulars, volunteers, rangers, or militia, who performed military service in any regiment, company, or detachment, in the service of the United States in the war with Great Britain, declared by the United States on the 18th day of June, 1812, or in any of the Indian wars since 1790, and each of the commissioned officers who was engaged in the military service of the United States in the late war with Mexico, shall be entitled to lands, as follows: Those who engaged to serve twelve months, or during the war, and actually served nine months, shall recive one hundred and sixty acres; and those who engaged to serve six months, and actually served four months, shall receive eighty acres; and those who engaged to serve for any, or an indefinite period, and actually served one month, shall receive forty acres; *Provided,* That wherever any officer or soldier was honorably discharged in consequence disability in the service before the expiration of his period of service, he shall receive the amount to which he would have been entitled if he had served the full period for which he had engaged to serve: *Provided,* the person so having been in service shall not receive said lands, or any part thereof, if it shall appear by the muster rolls of his regiment or corps that he deserted, or was dishonorably discharged from service, or if he has received, or is entitled to any military land bounty under any act of Congress heretofore passed.

SEC. 2. *And be it further enacted,* That the period during which any officer or soldier may have remained in captivity with the enemy shall be estimated and added to the period of his actual service, and the person so detained in captivity shall receive land under the provisions of this act in the same manner that he would be entitled in case he had entered the service for the whole term made up by the addition of the time of his captivity, and had served during such term.

SEC. 3. *And be it further enacted*, That each commissioned and non-commissioned officer, musician, or private, for whom provision is made by the first section hereof, shall receive a certificate, or warrant from the Department of the Interior for the quantity of land to which he may be entitled, and which may be located by the warrantee, or his heirs at law, at any land office of the United States, in one body, and in conformity to the legal sub-divisions of the public lands, upon any of the public lands in such district then subject to private entry: and upon the return of such certificate or warrant, with evidence of the location thereof having been legally made, to the General Land Office, a patent will be issued therefor. In event of the death of any commissioned or non-commissioned officer, musician, or private, prior or subsequent to the passage of this act, who shall have served as aforesaid, and who shall not have received bounty land for said services, a like certificate or warrant shall be issued in favor and to enure to the benefit of his widow, who shall receive one hundred and sixty acres of land, in case her husband was killed in battle, but not to her heirs: *Provided*, She is unmarried at the date of her application. *Provided further*, That no land warrant issued under the provisions of this act shall be laid upon any land of the United States to which there shall be a preemption right, or upon which there shall be an actual settlement and cultivation, except with the consent of such settler, to be satisfactorily proven to the proper land officer.

SEC. 4. *And be it further enacted*, That all sales, mortgages, letters of attorney, or other instruments of writing going to affect the title or claim to any warrant or certificate issued, or to be issued or any land granted, or to be granted, under the provisions of this act, made or executed prior to the issue, shall be null and void, to all intents and purposes whatsoever; nor shall such certificate or warrant, or the land obtained thereby, be in anywise affected by, or charged with, or subject to, the payment of any debt or claim incurred by such officer or soldier prior to the issuing of the patent: *Provided,* That the benefits of this act shall not accrue to any person who is a member of the present Congress: *Provided further,* That it shall be the duty of the Commissioner of the General Land Office, under such regulations as may be prescribed by the the Secretary of the Interior, to cause to be located, free of expense, any warrant which the holder may transmit to the General Land Office for that purpose, in such State and land district as the said holder or warrantee may designate, and upon good farming land, so far as the same can be ascertained from the maps, plats, and field notes from the surveyor, or from any other information in the possession of the land office; and upon the location being made, as aforesaid, the Secretary shall cause a patent to be transmitted to such warrantee: *And provided further,* That no patent issued under this act shall be delivered upon any power of attorney or agreement dated before the passage of this act; and that all such powers of attorney or agreements be considered and treated as null and void.—

Approved Sept. 28, 1850.

☞All claims under the aforesaid act should be addressed to the Commissioner of Pensions.

INSTRUCTIONS AND FORMS

To be observed by persons applying to the Pension Office for Bounty Land, under the Act of September 28th, 1850, entitled, "An Act granting Bounty Land to certain Officers and Soldiers who have been engaged in the military service of the "United States."

In every application for the benefit of the act aforesaid, whether made by the surviving officer or soldier himself, or by his widow or minor child or children, a declaration, under oath, must be made as nearly according to the following forms, as the nature of the case will admit.

Such declaration, and all affidavits, must be sworn to before some justice of the peace or other officer authorized to administer oaths for general purposes, who must certify the same.

The official character and signature of the magistrate who may administer the oath, must be certified by the clerk of the proper court of record of his county, under the seal of the court. *Such certificate must accompany every case.*

In every instance where the certificate of the certifying officer who authenticates the paper, is not written on the same sheet of paper which contains the affidavit or other papers authenticated, the certificate must be attached thereto by a piece of tape or narrow riband, the ends of which must pass under the official seal, so as to prevent any paper from being improperly attached to the certificate.

The 3d section, in express terms, only provides for the location of a warrant under the law. Thus the right to *locate* not being given to *an assignee*, the Department may well say that no assignments made prior to location will be recognized.

The 4th section declares, all sales, &c., going to affect the title to any *land*, granted or to be granted "prior to the issue," shall be null and void, and expressly declares, that the *land located* shall not be charged with or subject to any debt or claim "incurred prior to the issuing of the patent." It thus appears clear, that it was the intention of Congress that the claim of the soldier or his heirs, should continue free from every kind of incumbrance until after the *issue of the patent,* and thus relieve the Department from all the evils growing out of conflicting claims under alledged assignments.

The object of the law is to confer the right to the land itself on the warrantee or his heirs After that purpose is effected, it is of course competent for the grantee to dispose of it as he may think proper.

Form of a Declaration to be made by the surviving Officer or Soldier.

State of
} *ss.*
County of

On this day of A. D. one thousand eight hundred and , personally appeared before me, a Justice of the Peace, (*or other officer authorized to administer oaths for general purposes*) within and for the County and State aforesaid, aged years, a resident of in the State of , who being duly sworn according to law, declares, that he is the identical who was a in the Company* commanded by Captain in the Regiment of commanded by in the war with Great Britain declared by the United States on the 18th day of June, 1812, (*or other war embraced in said act, describing what war:*) that he enlisted (*or volunteered, or was drafted,*) at on or

*If the claimant was a regimental or staff officer, the declaration must be varied according to the facts of the case.

about the day of A. D. for the term of and continued in actual service in said war for the term of and was honorably discharged at on the day of A. D. , *as will appear by his original certificate of discharge herewith presented*,† or by the muster rolls of said company.

He makes this declaration for the purpose of obtaining the bounty land to which he may be entitled under the "act granting bounty land to certain officers and soldiers who have been engaged in the military service of the United States," passed September 28th, 1850.

(Signature of the claimant.)

Sworn to and subscribed before me the day and year above written. And I hereby certify, that I believe the said to be the identical man who served as aforesaid, and that he is of the age above stated.

(Signature of the magistrate or other officer.)

Form of a Declaration to be made by the Widow of a deceased Officer or Soldier.

State of } *ss.*
County of }

On this day of A. D. one thousand eight hundred and , personally appeared before me, a Justice of the Peace, (*or other officer authorized to administer oaths for general purposes*,) within and for the County and State aforesaid, aged years, a resident of in the State of who being duly sworn according to law, declares, that she is the widow of deceased, who was a in the Company commanded by Captain in the Regiment of commanded by in the war with Great Britain declared by the United States on the 18th day of June, 1812, (*or other war as the case may be*:) That her said husband enlisted (*or volunteered or was drafted*,) at on or about the day of A. D. for the term of and continued in actual service in said war, for the term of and was honorably discharged at on the

†If the discharge has been lost or destroyed, the words in *italics* will be omitted, and the facts in relation to the loss of the discharge stated in lieu thereof. If the claimant never received a written discharge, or if discharged in consequence of disability, or if he was in captivity with the enemy, he must vary his declaration, so as to set forth the facts of the case.

day of A. D. *as will appear by his original certificate of discharge herewith presented.**

She further states that she was married to the said
iu on the day of
A. D. by one a
and that her name before her said marriage was
that her said husband died at
on the day of A. D. , and
that she is still a widow.

She makes this declaration for the purpose of obtaining the bounty land to which she may be entitled under the "act passed September 28th, 1850.

(Claimant's Signature.)

Sworn to and subscribed before me the day and year above written.

(Officer's Signature.)

*The notes to the preceding declaration are also applicable to this. In some cases it will, perhaps, be impossible for the wibow to state the facts, in relation to her husband's services, with the particularity as to dates &c., indicated by the above form. In such case she must set forth the facts with as much accuracy as possible. It will be *indispensable* for her to state the Company and Regiment in which he served. If her husband was killed in battle, that fact must be set forth in the declaration.

This declaration must be accompanied by satisfactory proof of the marriage, and of the husband's death. If there is any public record of the marriage, a duly certified copy of such record should be forwarded if possible. If there is no public record of the marriage, but a private or family record, such family record, or a certified copy of the same, should be forwarded, with the affidavit of some disinterested person, proving the genuineness of the original, and that the copy certified is a true and correct copy of it. If no public or private record of the marriage exists, or can be procured, that fact should be set forth in the declaration; and in such case, other evidence, such as the testimony of persons who knew the parties in the lifetime of the husband, and knew them to live together as husband and wife, and to be so reputed, will be admissible.

☞In no case, however, will the mere statement of witnesses, that the claimant *is the widow* of the deceased, be taken as evidence of the marriage; but the witnesses must state the *facts* and *circumstances* from which they derive their knowledge or opinion that she is the widow of the deceased.

A certificate from the clergyman or magistrate, who solemnized the marriage is not competent evidence, unless the genuineness of the certificate be proved, and the person who gave it be shewn to have been authorized to solemnize marriages.

APPLICATIONS BY MINOR CHILDREN.

If any officer or soldier who would be entitled to bounty land under said act, if living, has died, leaving no widow who still survives him, but leaving a child or children under the age of majority, at the time of the passage of said act, such minor child or children are entitled to the same quantity of land that the father would be entitled to if living.

In such case the *guardian* of such minor child or children must make a declaration as nearly corresponding with the foregoing forms as the nature of the case will admit. He must state the time of the father's death; the fact that no widow survives him; and must state the *name* or *names*, and *exact age* or *ages* of his surviving minor child or children.

This declaration must be accompanied by *satisfactory proof* of the father's death, that no widow survives him, of the ages of the minor children, and of his own appointment, by competent authority, as guardian. If there is any *family record* showing the ages of the children, it or a certified copy of the same, should be forwarded, with the affidavit of some disinterested person, proving the genuineness of the original, and that the copy certified is a true and correct copy of it.

NOTICE TO BOUNTY LAND CLAIMANTS.

DEPARTMENT OF THE INTERIOR,
Washington, October 31, 1850.

Applicants for bounty land, or for information in relation thereto, are requested to address their communicatons on that subject to the Commissioner of Pensions direct. Their transmission through the Department proper imposes on it a very great and unnecessary amount of labor, and the additional examination they must thereby necessarily undergo, only creates delay, and increases their liability to be lost or mislaid.

Whenever new questions arise under the law, the decision of the Department will be communicated to the Commissioner of Pensions, and he will thereby be enabled, as he is required to do, promptly to acknowledge the receipt of all communications, and answer such inquiries as may be made.

As numerous inquiries have been directed to those points, it may be well to state—

1st. That where the service has been rendered by a *substitute*, he is the person entitled the benefit of the law, and not his employer.

2d. That the widow of a soldier who has rendered the service required by the law is entitled to bounty land, provided she was a widow at the passage of the law, although she may have been married a second time; but if not a widow at that time the benefit of the act inures to the minor children of the deceased soldier.

3d. That no person, who had received or is entitled to bounty land under a prior law, is entitled to the benefit of the act of 28th September, 1850.

4th. That no soldier is entited to more than one warrant under this act, although he may have served several terms; but where a soldier has served several terms, he will receive a warrant for the greatest quantity of land to which those several terms, consolidated, will entitle him.

ALEX. H. H. STUART,
Secretary of the Interior.

By a circular letter emanating from the Commissioner of Pensions, it seems that the Marine Corps, who were embodied in the field and performed service as a portion of the line of the army, are entitled. This rule we suppose will include a number of both officers and men, who served in the war with Great Britain and in the Indian war in Florida.

LOCATION OF WARRANTS.

The inquiries are numerous, how is the process of location to be accomplished? There are two modes. The claimant must decide in what land district, in which there are public lands subject to entry, he will have the location made. He may then in person, or by an agent near the land office, or sent for that purpose, examine all such land, make the entry, and delivering up the land warrant to the Register and Receiver, take from them their certificate of his entry. Upon this certificte the General Land Office, upon receiving it, will proceed to issue the patent. Or he may send his warrant directly to the General Land Office, and the Commissioner, by writing, to the land officers of the district he may elect and indicate, will cause the location and entry to be made, and the certificate to be returned to him for the patent. In the former mode of location, of course, there will be some expense involved, and in both there will be more or less uncertainty of getting good or even fair land, but the inducements, or the objections to the one mode or the other, will readily occur to every one, and each warrantee, if the decision of the Secretary is maintained, must make his own calculation, and form his own judgment and conclusion, between the two, for himself.

COPIES OF ROLLS.

A notion has extensively prevailed that all the muster rolls in possesion of the Government would be printed, and copies transmttted to the county clerks, to enable parties to make out their claims. If such a purpose was at any time in view, it is certainly now abandoned. The rolls are not to be printed, and it is clear from the letters of the Commissioner of Pensions, the 3d Auditor, and the Adjutant General, that applications must first be made before an examination can take place—to find the proof of the service upon which it depends. The Department is desirous to avail itself of the statement of the claimant himself, and to derive conclusions for or against the claim, from its agreement or discordance with the evidence of the rolls. Every claimant must therefore first make his declaration. Exact accuracy, in every particular, is not to be expected, but the leading points of the declaration must not only be capable of documentary authentication, but must serve as a clue to the proper company or regimental roll to be examined. Without this clue, no examination will be made, or if it be materially erroneous, the examination will be fruitless. The utmost particularity should be observed in giving the name of the captain or other officer under whom, the description of the troops in which, and as near as possible the time when, the service was rendered.

The rolls prior to 1812, it seems, are not in existence. In cases arising prior to 1812, the declaration should be as full and circumstantial as possible, aud be accompanied by the testimony of two witnesses to the service alledged.

Every case should be, in itself, both complete and exclusive. It should not include a claim for any other allowance, and should not depend on papers filed in another case. Oaths may be administered by a notary public, and in that case, the certificate of the clerk is not required, provided the seal of the notary annexed has a device or inscription to distinguish it from others.

The Commissioner of Pensions has given notice, that all claims will be taken up in the order in which they are received in his office. His first step is to send the particulars of the declaration to the office which has in its possession the proper roll, and upon return of the proof it affords, he proceeds to decide. If he decide in favor of the claim, he issues a land warrant, which is sent to the Commissioner of the General Land Office, who registers, countersigns, and delivers or transmits it, to the person authorized to receive it This warrant, by the decision of the Department, is not assignable. The owner, by such decision, can make no use of it, or of the land for which it is issued, until the warrant is located and a patent is issued therefor.

www.ingramcontent.com/pod-product-compliance
Lightning Source LLC
LaVergne TN
LVHW021428110826
845150LV00007B/2135